Praise for *Too Blessed to Be Stressed*

· ·

❧ Dealing with unrealistic expectations and with that stun-gunned-in-the-forehead kind of stress? *Too Blessed to Be Stressed* is a fun-filled read overflowing with insights and practical tips. Perfectly delicious for living happily ever after!

—Rhonda Rhea, www.RhondaRhea.org
Bestselling author of *Whatsoever Things Are Lovely*

❧ Deb's new book, *Too Blessed to Be Stressed*, will have you laughing so hard you'll wonder what it was you were stressed about in the first place. Debbie's humorous take on life, her clever way with words, and her well-honed skill of bringing the reader into her zany world is worth four times the price of this book. They say you can't buy happiness, but you can sure buy a couple hundred pages of laughs, and they're right here!

—Martha Bolton
Emmy-nominated writer and author of over eighty books, including
Didn't My Skin Used to Fit? and
The Whole World's Changing and I'm Too Hot to Care

❧ *Too Blessed to Be Stressed*, Debora Coty's delightful collection of wit and humor, is written in Coty's distinctive style and humorous approach to the stresses of our daily lives. An inspiring read that leaves you laughing, crying, and truly blessed.

—Ruth Carmichael Ellinger
Award-winning author of the Wildrose Inspirational series

❧ Deb Coty has a way of drawing you in and making you feel as if you're swapping stories with your best friend. She's a gifted writer who understands womanhood in all its pain and glory. *Too Blessed to Be Stressed* invites readers to embrace God's grace as they cope with life and its sticky messes.

—Suzanne Woods Fisher
Bestselling author of *The Choice* and
Amish Peace: Simple Wisdom for a Complicated World

Scripture quotations marked NIV are taken from the HOLY BIBLE, NEW INTERNATIONAL VERSION®. NIV®. Copyright 1973, 1978, 1984, 2011 by Biblica, Inc.™ Used by permission. All rights reserved worldwide.

Scripture quotations marked CEV are from the Contemporary English Version, Copyright © 1995 by American Bible Society. Used by permission.

Scripture quotations marked KJV are taken from the King James Version of the Bible.

Scripture quotations marked NASB are taken from the New American Standard Bible, © 1960, 1962, 1963, 1968, 1971, 1972, 1973, 1975, 1977, 1995 by The Lockman Foundation. Used by permission.

Scripture quotations marked MSG are taken from *THE MESSAGE*. Copyright © by Eugene H. Peterson 1993, 1994, 1995, 1996, 2000, 2001, 2002. Used by permission of NavPress Publishing Group.

Scripture quotations marked NLT are taken from the *Holy Bible*. New Living Translation copyright© 1996, 2004, 2007 by Tyndale House Foundation. Used by permission of Tyndale House Publishers, Inc. Carol Stream, Illinois 60188. All rights reserved.

Published in association with the literary agency of WordServe Literary Group, Ltd., www.wordserveliterary.com.

Published by Shiloh Run Press, an imprint of Barbour Publishing, Inc., P.O. Box 719, Uhrichsville, Ohio 44683, www.barbourbooks.com

Our mission is to publish and distribute inspirational products offering exceptional value and biblical encouragement to the masses.

 Member of the
Evangelical Christian
Publishers Association

Printed in China.

Too Blessed
to be
Stressed

Debora M. Coty

A JOURNAL

SHILOH RUN PRESS
An Imprint of Barbour Publishing, Inc.

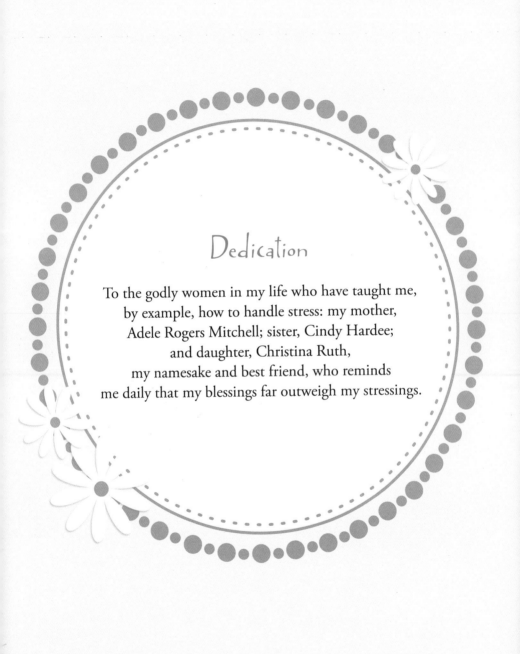

Dedication

To the godly women in my life who have taught me,
by example, how to handle stress: my mother,
Adele Rogers Mitchell; sister, Cindy Hardee;
and daughter, Christina Ruth,
my namesake and best friend, who reminds
me daily that my blessings far outweigh my stressings.

Contents

Introduction

So, girl, are you feeling the pulse throb in your temples as the spike in blood pressure melts your earrings? Are you as busy as the proverbial one-armed wallpaper hanger? Is *frenzy* too tame a word for the hair-ripping, hand-trembling anxiety that keeps your heart in a vise and your humor imprisoned by the joy-sucking dully-funks?

Welcome to the slightly frazzled sisterhood that shares your distress about stress. With the hectic lifestyles we lead in these unpredictable times, we just can't seem to avoid worrying about choking finances, impossible schedules, unstable health issues, or a myriad of other stressors that steal our peace.

My goal in writing *Too Blessed to Be Stressed* is to help you rejuvenate your desperate heart by discovering simple-to-implement, practical ways to attain that peace we all crave. The peace that passes all understanding. The amazing, empowering peace that enables us to actually *feel* blessed in the delirium of the fray.

Together, let's learn creative coping techniques and calm our fretful spirits through bite-sized, digestible doses of the Bread of Life. Maybe a hunk of Godiva, too!

Above all, I want to remind you how to laugh. A real, honest-to-goodness, gurgling-from-the-guts giggle. The kind that acts as a catalyst to release the joy of the Lord in your soul and color your future with hope for a better tomorrow.

"A cheerful heart is good medicine, but a crushed spirit dries up the bones" (Proverbs 17:22 NIV). C'mon, sister, open wide and let's take our medicine!

Love,
Deb

Section 1:
Time Management

PRESSURE CREATES BOTH
DIAMONDS AND VOLCANOES

*Good judgment comes from
bad experiences and a lot of that
comes from bad judgment.*
UNKNOWN

Superwoman Has Left the Building
—HEALTH AWARENESS—

*The LORD said, "I will go with
you and give you peace."*
EXODUS 33:14 CEV

Kick back a moment and take this revealing true-or-false stress test
for women:

☐T ☐F   I am frequently grumpy and I don't know why.

☐T ☐F   I used to enjoy cooking, but now it's only
a necessary chore.

☐T ☐F   I don't feel appreciated for all the tasks that I do.

☐T ☐F   I'm embarrassed if caught relaxing or being
"unproductive."

☐T ☐F   The volume of my voice increases to MAKE MY POINT!

☐T ☐F   I feel like I live in my car.

☐T ☐F   I can't remember the last time I laughed till I cried.

☐T ☐F   A "free" day is exhausting because I must complete all my home duties.

☐T ☐F   I tend to eat when feeling tense or overwhelmed.

☐T ☐F   I feel like I'm constantly on the defensive.

☐T ☐F   I often have unexplained headaches or stomachaches.

☐T ☐F   My to-do lists have footnotes.

Now count the answers that you marked "true" and check out your status:
4–6: Yellow Alert! You are at risk of becoming stressed out.
7–9: Orange Alert! Look out, girlfriend, you're at toxic stress levels.
10–12: Red Alert!!! You are a bonified *Stress Mess* and need immediate help!

Surprised? I certainly was when I took the test.

But we really shouldn't be stunned if we're tuned in to ourselves. Stress overload symptoms don't appear overnight. When our computers begin to freeze up, we recognize that it's time to turn off and reboot. When the warning light shines on the car dashboard, we wouldn't dream of ignoring it. When the bathroom scale pointer begins to spin like a fan, we know it's time to ditch the brownies.

If we ignore the signs, stress will eventually take a toll on our bodies.

We women tend to internalize stress. We take confrontation and subtle discord very personally. Heated words and even mild disagreements often sink into our innards, depositing a sense of unsettledness and anxiety. When we can't find an outlet for our pent-up frustration, we sometimes resort to self-destructive behavior. We eat too much. We smoke. We drink. We abuse our bodies. We may even isolate ourselves.

We're only deceiving ourselves if we think our loved ones don't notice the external signs of our inner distress—fussing, fuming, and fatigue. I call them the Three Fs. We may not even realize how far we've sunk in the stress-pool until those who care about us point it out, usually by evidence of the Three Fs: outward fussing, inward fuming, and chronic fatigue.

I knew it was time to address my stress issues when my growl grew louder than the dog's and my fam tactfully suggested I get a rabies shot.

But listen, it's what we don't see, the below-the-surface stress symptoms, that are the scariest. Cortisol, a hormone our bodies release in the grip of stress, contributes to out-of-control feelings of helplessness and hopelessness. Studies confirm that over time, stress increases blood pressure, contributes to migraines and tension headaches, and results in the plaque that leads to coronary artery and heart disease. Chronic stress has been found to increase cardiovascular risk by up to 50 percent! Not to mention documented ties to ulcers, asthma, insomnia,

strokes, cancer, obesity, depression, anxiety attacks, colds, flu, and alcoholism.

And those crying jags when you're frazzled? Not coincidence. Stress lowers estrogen production, which can trigger emotional outbursts. You know, without our hormones we're bubbling volcanoes waiting to erupt.

Am I describing you? If so, please allow me to speak as your new BFF: honey, put on your big-girl panties and face facts. You are *not* Superwoman with nerves of steel. Or guts either. Stress is kryptonite, and it's out to rip off your cape and reduce you to a pile of quivering, ineffective mush.

Okay, that's the bad news. How about some good news?

Take a deep breath. Close your eyes. Exhale slowly. There. You've just taken the first step in stress reduction. There are plenty of simple but effective techniques for boosting our body's stress resilience:

- Add yourself to your daily to-do list. Schedule fifteen minutes twice a day to revive, regroup, and regenerate. Remove yourself from the stress source, even if it means just stepping outside for a few minutes. (I walk laps around the parking lot at work or swing on a hammock in the backyard at home.) Air out your brain. Sing along to your favorite CD. Read an inspirational novel or a magazine. Whatever helps you chill. And don't take no for an answer when other activities try to crowd *you* out. You're important!

- Take laugh breaks. Lighten up, sister! "The joy of the LORD is your strength" (Nehemiah 8:10 NIV)! Some say Christians should be sober and serious and silent as the grave, but I say Jesus came *out* of the grave and that's the best reason in the world to celebrate!

- Relax your knotted muscles with five-minute stress-busters throughout the day. Stop thinking. Get physical! Stretch, bend, roll those tense shoulders (more great relaxation stretches in chapter 29), chase the dog—get that reinvigorating blood flowing through your body tissues as your wasted mind takes a break. Crank up the praise music while you do housework: line dance while vacuuming, swing dance while cooking, boogie with the grocery cart in the frozen food aisle. Movement causes your brain to secrete beta-endorphin, which helps calm and de-stress you. You'll need that for the checkout line.

- Immerse your weariness. Try a Jacuzzi, if available, a bubble bath up to your chin, dipping in a cool spring, or floating in a relaxing pool. Even just standing in the shower, away from the world, can help wash away exhaustion and rejuvenate gasping body tissues (including brain cells). *Feel* the moment and focus on the water's refreshing sensory input to your skin; allow it to spread buoyancy to your spirit.

- Repetitive redundancy. No, this is not the name of a new rock group. It's what you should do to take your frantic self down a notch: crochet, do needlepoint, play piano scales, rock out (we're talking about a rocking chair here, not retro Joan Jett) to soothing sounds like chirping birds or a babbling fountain (get a table model for your porch or den—I *love* mine, except for the fact that listening to all that running water makes me flee to the bathroom). You need a calm, repetitive, manual task that takes minimal brainpower. Chopping firewood doesn't count.

- Ask for help! Delegate responsibilities and chores. Hire help if you can afford it. If you can't, beg. I have a wonderful, organizationally gifted girlfriend who wades in once a month to keep my house from turning into a nuclear waste site (love you, Teresa!). The rest of the time, chores are divided between family members. If everyone does their part, no one is left exhausted.

- Give up perfectionism. Ain't nobody perfect but Jesus, and you're not Him. Let a few things go. Tomorrow, release a few more. In time those tasks will quit nagging at you, and you'll literally feel the stress rocks in your stomach disintegrate into dust.

So when those stress overload signs start popping up and the red cape threatens to sprout over our blue tights, um. . .I mean, jeans, let's do ourselves a favor and remind each other that we don't have to perpetuate the myth of Superwoman. She's left the building and lost the key!

Half our life is spent trying to find something to do with the time we have rushed through life trying to save.

WILL ROGERS

Let's Decom-stress

1. Which questions on the stress test rated your strongest "true"? Do you ever demonstrate the Three Fs to your family? When and why?

2. So what can you do about it? Which stress resilience technique will you implement and in what specific way? (You don't have to stick with the suggestions I've made. Creatively tailor a technique to your unique situation.)

Martha on Steroids
—Setting Priorities—

*Let all things be done
decently and in order.*

1 Corinthians 14:40 KJV

Are you a filer or a piler? Do you file things away in their proper places and organize your home in delightful Martha Stewart fashion? Or do you leave little piles all over like shrines to the clutter god, which eventually turn into lurching Stonehenge precipices that threaten to avalanche and bury your living room?

I tend to be a little of both. You'll rarely find crumbs beside my toaster; just don't look underneath. A pair of dust bunnies may dance in the dining room, but whole squads play hockey with the roaches beneath the beds. Cat hair tumbleweeds aren't usually rolling down the hallway; just don't sit on the couch wearing black pants. A few grimy corners may grace the tub, but you'll never be privy to them. Hey, that's what shower curtains are for.

Housework is something nobody notices until you ignore it. Then *everybody* becomes your mother: Do you live in a barn? I don't remember an indoor blizzard! I forget—what color is this carpet?

So I'm not Martha Stewart. Or even the biblical Martha who zipped around cleaning, cooking, and organizing when the Son of God came to visit (see Luke 10:38–42). But isn't that a good thing? Didn't Jesus rebuke Martha for her preoccupation as a human *do*-ing rather than a human *be*-ing?

I'm neat, but not immaculate. Orderly, but not obsessed. Clean enough for health, dirty enough for happiness. And I'm not alone.

"Clean enough" seems to be the new mantra sweeping our bustlingly busy country as women find little time for once-sacred housekeeping duties. I understand that an average of 26.5 hours per week was spent housecleaning in 1965 compared to 17 hours today. The latter is roughly 2.4 hours per day.

In Coty math (read: not reproducible), that means we're picking up something every 12 minutes!

Four decades ago the scouring, of course, would have been performed mostly by women, the majority of whom didn't work outside the home and considered their sparkling terrazzo a reflection of personal worth. Thankfully, menfolk do more these days. The Council on Contemporary Families reports that the masculine contribution to household duties has doubled in the past fifty years, and help with child care has tripled.

I can't complain there. The good Lord blessed me with a 50-50 husband. Well, since writing began devouring my spare time, his share has burgeoned to more like 75 percent. Hey, I'm not vain. I'll admit he's a much better scrubber than me. I'm a lick-and-a-promise gal, but he's into minute details, and since he took over, my gleaming pot bottoms double as NASA solar reflectors. Our polka-dot carpet turned out to be tan. There's actually a face behind all the toothpaste flicks on the bathroom mirror.

I don't even refer to the kitchen sink as "The Promised Land" anymore. On a trip to Israel, we learned that excavation down through layers of previous civilizations' left-behind refuse reveals interesting facets of history. Hey, I could do the same thing with the food layers coating my sink. Want to know how many potatoes I peeled for Easter dinner in 2006?

Look, it's not my fault. Who can withstand the relentless forces of spontaneous degeneration, one of the biggest stressors of domesticated life? Never heard of that infamous Coty near-fact of science? Took me years of dedicated observation and study to discover the reason my house looks like it does. Please, let me enlighten you.

The theory of spontaneous degeneration declares that when left in an unnaturally clean state, matter will spontaneously atrophy into indiscriminant disarray.

You, too, have witnessed the ravages of spontaneous degeneration: an hour after you triumphantly finish slaving over a clean house, mold begins sprouting on shiny faucets, green slime oozes from the vegetable crisper, tiny hairs creep

up from the drain and embed themselves in the bathroom sink, and dust bunnies proliferate for a closet reunion.

Black dirt erupts like lava from the carpet nap, clothing magically appears on every piece of sit-able furniture, dirty panties peek from behind hampers just in time for the dog to proudly present them to dinner guests. And most mysterious of all, pairs of clean wet socks innocently entering the dryer become tragically widowed as their mates are magically transported to the parallel universe of the Pogo People, who hop around on one foot wearing Junior's sports high-tops.

Housekeeping is a perpetual lesson in futility. Cleaning an occupied house is like combing your hair in a hurricane.

The way I see it, I'm actually being thoughtful by ignoring my mop and dust rag. I'm eliminating the sinful temptation for friends who might fall short in comparison. In fact, they've learned to appreciate my dust decor and even occasionally leave cute little DON'T EAT HERE messages finger-etched on the coffee table.

I *try* to clean up, but sometimes my efforts backfire. Like the south Florida woman who accidentally rammed an alligator with her car. Seriously. She dutifully cleaned up the road but crashed into a parked car when the possum-playing gator began thrashing around in her backseat. The poor dear was charged with a felony: possession of an alligator. (We can't count votes down here, but we're sure on top of illegal reptiles!)

So when we're tempted to forsake our devotional moments, family time, or prayer walks to toothbrush the grout, disinfect the toilets, or scrub the baseboards like Martha on steroids, let's remember Jesus' words to His beloved spiritual sister: "Martha, dear Martha, you're fussing far too much and getting yourself worked up over nothing" (Luke 10:41 MSG).

Only one thing is truly of eternal importance: Papa God. And He created dirt.

My second favorite household chore is ironing.
My first being hitting my head on the top
bunk bed until I faint.

ERMA BOMBECK

LET'S DECOM-STRESS

1. Take a moment to read the story of Mary and Martha in Luke 10:38–42. With which sister can you most identify? Why?

2. How do you think the stress levels differ for a Martha, who rushes about cleaning and cooking to perfection, and a Mary, who makes time to sit at the feet of Jesus and soak in His presence?

3. Rearrange the following priorities in order of importance to you: "me" time, family, faith, work, achieving success, appearance, relationships, schedules. On which three do you spend the most time?

4. Which are of eternal value? Do you feel the need to make any changes in your priorities?

Can I Hear Me Now?
—SELF-TALK—

*If our minds are ruled by our desires,
we will die. But if our minds are ruled by
the Spirit, we will have life and peace.*

ROMANS 8:6 CEV

"I just *cannot* learn this new system."

"That's impossible!"

"There's no way I'll ever get along with her."

Have you ever spouted loaded statements like these birthed from frustration? If you're like me, they're typical of your speech during a single day. Sometimes a single hour. But what impact does this type of self-talk really have when we make such sweeping, absolute declarations?

My tennis coach, Pete, used to stop cold in the middle of a drill when he sensed my negative attitude beginning to rear its ugly head. It was probably my primal scream and the way I slammed my racket into the net that tipped him off.

"I can't make this shot!" I'd seethe through gritted teeth after the tenth straight drop shot into the net. "Just forget it! I. Am. Not. Able. I won't keep wasting time on something that will *never* happen."

Pete, in his calm, nonjudgmental way, would turn his palms upward, shrug his shoulders, and say, "Debbie, what are you telling yourself?"

"Only the facts," I'd mutter, stubbornly refusing to acknowledge his point.

"Ah, but facts change. If you tell yourself, 'I can't,' then it's a fact that you won't. Ever. But if you tell yourself, 'I haven't yet, but with a few minor adjustments, I will,' that becomes an even stronger fact and it supersedes the first."

He was right, of course, and proof was in the wicked drop shot I eventually developed after a mere four thousand more tries.

Positive self-talk isn't just crucial in sports; it's a *huge* part of everyday stress management. When we tell ourselves something over and over, we eventually buy into it, and it becomes a part of our inner makeup, our self-esteem, our performance motivation—for better or worse. In essence, we choose our attitude and that attitude dictates our stress level.

"Okay, that first soufflé flopped, but so did Julia Child's. I'll make a few adjustments and the next one will be the chef d'oeuvre." By choosing an upbeat attitude, our outlook becomes much more optimistic and consequently less stress-producing.

The trouble is that we often don't recognize we're engaging in negative self-talk. Negativity is habit-forming. We unconsciously develop a compromised view of ourselves when we consistently think things like, "I'm such a loser," "This is too hard," or "Why even try?"

Channeling Eeyore becomes the soundtrack for our subconscious thoughts. Those mopey, self-depreciating donkey thoughts wear us down and wear us out before we even realize the source of erosion. We're actually sabotaging ourselves. We settle for defeat when, with a few minor attitude adjustments, we could open the door for amazing possibilities.

Pessimism affects us physically as well as mentally and emotionally. Negativity has a direct correlation to heart disease, immune system deficits, and our ability to cope with physical pain. A thirty-year Mayo Clinic study of eight hundred patients revealed that pessimists' risk of early death was 19 percent higher than that of optimists. Dr. Martin Seligman of the University of Pennsylvania concludes, "Optimism and pessimism affect health almost as clearly as do physical factors."

The worst part of negative self-talk is that we're not only limiting ourselves; we're limiting our God. The Creator of the universe. The One who is ready to fill us with expectancy and hope and potential and wants us to instead tell ourselves, "I can do *everything* through Christ, who gives me strength" (Philippians 4:13 NLT, emphasis mine).

So is the glass half empty or only half the calories?

How do we reboot ourselves with a fresh perspective and, in the process, significantly reduce the strain and drain produced by negative self-talk?

- Cut and paste. We must train ourselves to recognize negative inner chatter the minute it starts and delete immediately. Shake the mental Etch-A-Sketch. Get out the attitude chain saw. It helps me to make a "time out" signal with my hands as a physical cue. But don't stop there. Replace those negative thoughts with a positive spin. Let's transpose the negative self-talk at the beginning of this chapter as an example:

    "What can I do to learn this new system?"

    "How can I break down this mammoth task into small, doable steps?"

    "I've learned to get along with my mother-in-law. I can learn to get along with anybody."

- Tweak your tone. You know how your doctor says, "This may pinch a little," as he jams the needle into your arm? Borrow his technique and reduce big ugly *blackhead* wordage to smaller, unintimidating *blemish* terms. "Impossible" is a brick wall compared to "this may take some work." Wouldn't you rather tackle a project that's "challenging" rather than "unmanageable"?

- Be your own BFF (Blessed Friend Forever). Using your BFF voice, intentionally over-dub that Eeyore voice droning inside. Speak to yourself like you would your very best friend. Make it a point to be encouraging, uplifting, affirming, light, and humorous (you'll listen better!).

- Avoid comparisons. Everyone has a different skill set. You are unique. The way you do things may differ from the techniques of others, but that doesn't make it wrong. To quote my granddaddy (and yours): "There's more than one way to skin a cat." (Try not to imagine how that adage originated!) Self-inflicted competition is unfair and only fosters more negativity. Unless you're the reigning world champion, there will always be someone better than you at a specific skill. So what? You don't need another tiara.

- Be creative. Open your mind to new possibilities. Pretend you're Michael Jordan and belt out, "I believe I can fly. . ." Okay, skip the MJ part but, really, solutions are only found by those who search for them.

- Memorize Philippians 4:13. Repeat frequently. Trust God and act on it!

✿ Tack on hope. Add that magical three-letter word, *yet*. When tacked on at the end of a negative thought, it miraculously transforms "I can't" perspectives into "I can with a little more time." The difference is subtle but profound:

"I can't make this work. . .yet."

"I'm not smart enough to figure this out. . .yet."

"I'm not handling this well. . .yet."

See? With one word, you've just added instant hope, girlfriend!

✿ Act positive to actually become positive. In his book *Winning the Stress Challenge*, Dr. Nick Hall cites a study he conducted proving that signals transmitted to a person's brain when she's behaving a certain way provoke similar physical and mental changes to those elicited by real emotional responses. In other words, putting on a happy-face mask truly makes us feel happier!

We believe and internalize what we tell ourselves. Words are powerful. They have the ability to change our perception of our own abilities from limited to limitless. It's incredible how much difference a little optimism makes in reducing everyday stress. Everything looks surprisingly brighter, warmer, more hopeful.

Positive self-talk is not a new concept. We just need to pick up what the apostle Paul put down in Philippians 4:8: "Fix your thoughts on what is true, and honorable, and right, and pure, and lovely, and admirable. Think about things that are excellent and worthy of praise" (NLT).

And keep going after those drop shots!

Whether you think you can or think you can't—you are right.

HENRY FORD

Let's Decom-stress

1. When do you most often engage in negative self-talk? What do you tell yourself?

2. Think a moment about the top three negative messages you routinely send yourself. Now practice tweaking your tone, speaking like your own BFF, and tacking on hope. Go ahead—practice your new positive messages aloud. Remember these transposition statements next time you begin sliding down the slippery slope of negativity! Take the bold step from negative to positive thinking!

3. Meditate for five minutes on Philippians 4:13. What is God saying to you through this scripture?

....
....
....
....
....
....
....
....
....
....
....
....

Shoving the Envelope
—FINDING BALANCE—

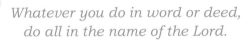

Whatever you do in word or deed,
do all in the name of the Lord.

COLOSSIANS 3:17 NASB

Enthusiasm is a good thing, right? We *should* be passionate about things we feel strongly about. But are there limits, even to passion? Is there a fine line to avoid crossing when gusto begins to tangle our nerves instead of soothe them?

My health-food nut husband, Chuck, was absolutely thrilled with his new handy dandy juicer. This was not just your average, everyday juicer. This puppy could pretty much suck down the entire contents of our refrigerator in one gulp and spit out a vat of thick, gray, disgusting-looking, but oh-so-healthy juice within seconds.

Chuck got his jollies in demonstrating his new toy to everyone who so much as planted a toe within 100 yards of our house. Like Tim "The Tool Man" Taylor, he took great pride in morphing into Chuck "The Juice Man" Coty, repeatedly constructing and dismantling the stainless steel monster and revving the mega-horsepower motor that sounded like a rocket launcher.

After a while, he began experimenting with various juice concoctions. His goal was to create that ultimate lifetime accomplishment: the healthiest, power-packed liquid food known to man.

So instead of juicing five organic carrots with a few apples for breakfast, he added a whole pound of carrots. Instead of a smidge of carrot flavor with his mixed greens and beet lunch innovation, he crammed an entire grocery store carrot display into the machine and out gushed a river of orange sludge.

After three weeks of this ultra-healthy diet, one night at Bible study, I noticed our friend Sharon, a registered nurse, staring at Chuck. She didn't take her eyes off him, even through prayer time. After the last amen, she pulled me aside and whispered, "Has Chuck had a checkup lately? I think his liver may be malfunctioning."

"*What?*" I nearly shouted in surprise. "Why would you think that?"

"Well, just look at him. He's so jaundiced, he glows."

We both turned to gawk. Sure enough, Chuck's skin was the color of a shining jack-o-lantern. I don't know how I hadn't noticed before. Worried, I motioned for Chuck to join us in a secluded corner, and Sharon shared her dire concerns.

To my astonishment, Chuck burst into laughter as Sharon and I looked helplessly at each other. "It's the carrots," he explained between guffaws. "Gotta be the carrots. Too much beta carotene. Must have spilled over into my system."

Thankfully, as he trimmed his carrot intake during the following month, he looked less and less like a steroidal tangerine. Foiled in his first attempt, he decided to try, try again to create the world's healthiest smoothie.

I've been taking garlic tablets for years, he thought. (He tells me it's a superb antifungal agent.) *What if I add fresh garlic to my juice?*

A fine notion, perhaps, but he forgot one thing. Processed garlic tablets are odorless. And very small. Can you see where we're headed here?

So, following the Tim Taylor line of reasoning that if a little is good, a lot is better, one fine morning Chuck crammed three whole cloves of garlic down the juicer chute along with his usual bushel of produce. He happily downed the concoction and naively returned to work at his computer.

Have you ever seen a picture of Hiroshima?

That's what happened in his stomach about ten minutes later. And the gift kept on giving. Garlic exploded out through every possible exit of his body for the next two weeks. When he wasn't groaning in the bathroom, his loving family reaped the consequences of his ill-fated health experiment. Besides eye-watering belches and, um, potent flatulence (is there a nice word for this?), garlic odor oozed out of every wretched pore and encompassed him in a toxic cloud like that of Charlie Brown's filthy bud, Pigpen.

When I vowed "For better or worse" at my wedding, I had no clue how diverse "worse" could be. Instead of just pushing the envelope, my husband was shoving it.

But food isn't the only realm where extremes aren't healthy. As a young mom, I thought *give your all to God* meant "hop till you drop."

On Sundays, God's designated day of rest and worship, I'd awaken at dawn; nurse, bathe, dress the baby; rouse the rest of the fam; feed, clothe, and herd them to the car; then run back inside to change the baby and myself after the diaper leaked all over my dress. Then at church, I'd drop everyone off in their proper locations, trot over to teach my third-grade Sunday school class, try to corral thirty choir kids to practice the spring musical, and dash over to the sanctuary in time to play piano for the 11:00 service.

Rest and worship were not on my agenda. By the time I arrived back home, I could only collapse on the couch in a stupor, useless to myself and my family on the day the Lord intended for us to rejuvenate the spirit and body. I was shoving my own envelope.

What about you? Are you overextending yourself? Spreading your time or energies too thin? Regardless of how well-intentioned we are, we're only human, and the Master Designer, who created us and *knows* our limitations, wants us to set parameters, to pick and choose the way we expend our finite energies.

To shove the envelope not only robs our joy and ability to live in the moment, but also steals fulfillment and effectiveness from the priorities God has appointed as our primary focus for this particular season of our life.

Do everything in moderation, including moderation.

BEN FRANKLIN

LET'S DECOM-STRESS

1. Name a time when you shoved the envelope by overextending yourself.

2. Consider Ecclesiastes 9:10: "Whatever your hand finds to do, do it with all your might" (NASB). Now contrast that verse with Psalm 62:5: "Yes, my soul, find rest in God; my hope comes from him" (NIV). How do you strike a healthy balance between activity and rest?

3. Think of ways you can do your best without going overboard in three specific areas of your life (e.g., church, home, work, marriage, parenting, self-expression, ministry, relationships, health management, etc.).

Papa God, Mama Earth
—DISCOVERING A DEEPER—
SHADE OF GREEN

*Generations come and generations go,
but the earth remains forever.*

ECCLESIASTES 1:4 NIV

Preserving the environment. We all want to do our part, right?

Maybe not exactly like the Beverly Hills liposuction doctor who tooled around town using *lipodiesel,* an alternate fuel he created from the discarded belly rolls, thunder thighs, and muffin tops of his clients.

Alas, the idea was short-lived. It seems that few of his fat donors were aware of their unique contribution toward energy conservation and weren't exactly thrilled about their cellulite touring the city without them. Besides, California law forbids using human waste to power vehicles. Go figure.

God is our Papa (in Old Testament Hebrew, *Abba,* the name for God, translates to the intimate form of "father," i.e., "daddy"), and He gave us (humankind) the honor of being caretakers of His glorious creation (see Genesis 1:26–28). In fulfilling this role, we are to show compassion, responsibility, and caring in our relationship with our earthly home and its other living residents. Yet many women report that an underlying stressor in their lives is the nagging worry that pollution and wanton wasting of our earth's natural resources will leave a destitute world for future generations. Additional stress is compiled by the helpless feeling that an individual can't make a difference.

Well, girl, I've got good news! There are plenty of simple ways we can glorify Papa God by respecting His creation and train our families to "lean green" in the process.

- Turn off lights, fans, and electrical gizmos when you leave the room, and power down your computer each night. TVs suck up about 10 percent of a home's electricity usage, so seriously reconsider whether Fido really needs to watch *Animal Kingdom* while you're at work. Small appliances (including cell phone chargers) tend to drain electricity when not in use, so unplug. I was surprised to learn that there is no significant residual cooling effect from running ceiling fans in unoccupied rooms, so only use them when you're present. And remember that the quarters it costs to run a lonesome lightbulb add up quickly.
- Replace incandescent lightbulbs with fluorescents, which can last up to ten times longer (and save around fifty dollars a year).
- Turn off your car engine while you wait; the old tale about using more gasoline to crank than to idle is hooey.
- Recycle glass, paper, cardboard, plastics, aluminum, and smiles. The latter lasts forever.
- You can recycle food, too, by slicing, processing, or stewing leftovers into a totally different form (e.g., a run through the food processor transforms bits and pieces of baked chicken into elegant chicken salad; leftover pork roast begets tasty barbecue). Another gastric re-gifting idea from the Coty kitchen: top recycled entrees with cheese, the culinary cure-all. If it's undercooked, mozzarella doubles as melted glue. Overcooked? Scrape off the burnt crust and pile on the sharp cheddar to disguise the charcoal taste. Tough as a saddle horn? Chop it up and drown it in Cheez Whiz. Just call me Wolfgang Coty.
- Become a dump cook. (No, not "dumb" cook, although my dinner guests may beg to differ.) To avoid excessive dishwashing (water, energy, pruney hands) and use fewer burners, dump everything together into one dish—meat, veggies, noodles (snooty cooks call it pasta), and occasionally salad greens or fruit if they'll fit in the pan. A clever cook can simultaneously serve all four Southern food groups: sweet, salty, fried, and au gratin. Successful dump cooking may take a little experimenting. Once I tried mango-spinach-turkey pizza. Even the dog turned up his nose.
- Start a compost pile or bin. For your mango-spinach-turkey pizza flops.

- Clean the dusty central air/heat filter regularly for energy efficiency, to purify the air, and pocket a few bucks.
- Conserve water. Replace toilets, faucets, and old showerheads with low-flow models. Repair leaky faucets that drip money and wasted gallons down the drain. Install sprinkler system rain sensors to avoid double dripping.
- Everyone likes a blankey. Tuck in your hot water heater with a precut, customized blanket to keep out the winter chill. Adjust the water temp to 120 degrees—plenty hot enough for cleaning dishes and clothes without threat of scalding tender tootsies.
- Speaking of insulation, check your attic and update ineffective insulation to conserve heating and A/C energy. Or adopt the Coty technique of stuffing your attic with mounds of useless junk that doubles as extra insulation!
- Buy reusable containers instead of cluttering up landfills with disposable plastic bags or bottles. We are, after all, creation's caretakers!
- Plant a backyard garden; reconnect with the practice of growing and consuming organic food. Kids who eat homegrown produce are much more likely than prepackaged-goodie-gorging young'uns to have better attitudes toward nutrition and healthy eating habits.
- Replace sections of that high-maintenance, water-guzzling lawn with drought-tolerant plants and shrubs that suck carbon from the atmosphere, emit refreshing oxygen, and are friendly with your ecosystem and climate. Install a backyard irrigation cistern that collects and distributes rainwater. Create a gorgeous landscape with less drain on the environment and your mowing energies.
- And my personal fave: ride a bike or walk instead of driving. It's a win-win! Biking in Papa God's beautiful outdoors burns calories (about 500 per hour) and clears out brain cobwebs. Plus, it saves gas and lowers our carbon-emissions footprint. I live within a five-mile radius of the post office and library, so whenever I need to mail packages, buy stamps, or return books, I hop on Ole Bess (my bicycle), secure the items in my basket (my kids call me Almira Gulch), and pedal up a happy sweat.

One small caveat: Beware of overzealous conservation efforts becoming stress-producers rather than stress-relievers. Anything good can be taken to bad extremes. I know a woman whose husband insists that she leave for work at the same time he does so the garage door opener is only used once each morning. Is the energy savings really worth the stress created by forcing her to arrive at work an hour early?

You know, I think our next national women's social reform project should be picketing our courthouses in favor of recycled cellulite gasoline. Better to set our cars in motion than our jiggling thighs, right? In the meantime, if we can't be fuel fat donors, at least we can run off natural sass!

So cheer up, sisters—we can all do *something* to help prevent wrinkles on the face of Mama Earth. Begin by taking the first baby step. After all, good planets are hard to find!

> We do not inherit the earth from our ancestors;
> we borrow it from our children.
>
> NATIVE AMERICAN PROVERB

LET'S DECOM-STRESS

1. List the ways your family currently "leans green."

2. What are two new conservation techniques that you feel led to implement? (Nope, you can't count cellulite fuel donations!)

3. Consider Genesis 8:22. How can we help in ensuring that the earth—our home away from our heavenly home—endures?

All Stressed Up and Nowhere to Break Down
—Coping with Loss—

He has never let you down,
never looked the other way when
you were being kicked around.
He has never wandered off to do his
own thing; he has been right there, listening.

PSALM 22:24 MSG

❧ The voice on the phone fades into oblivion as the forgotten instrument slowly drops from your quivering hand at 3:00 a.m.

❧ The slamming door sets your world spinning as if gravity has abandoned you, too.

❧ You hear but can't grasp the doctor's grave words as they tumble deep into a dark, cavernous pit inside your gut.

Bad news. Sudden devastating loss. Unexpected catastrophe.

It's true: We're all just one phone call from our knees. Shattering loss happens to all of us at some time in our lives. How do we deal with it? How do we get past the spiritual, physical, and emotional paralysis that often accompanies shock? How do we avoid complete and utter wipeout?

Please allow me to share successful coping skills from several godly women who have suffered life-altering losses.

After twenty-eight years of marriage, my friend Lauren's husband presented her with a pronouncement out of the blue: "I'm leaving you."

For years Lauren had struggled to hold down two jobs while simultaneously completing college courses to provide for their family of six when John could no longer work or drive due to a debilitating neurological disease. She chauffeured John to endless medical appointments and devotedly cared for her husband's special needs. Lauren was completely blindsided when John decided that she was somehow holding him back from getting well.

No one knows more than my friend Esther about desperately grasping the hope offered in 1 Corinthians 10:13 (MSG): "God will never let you down; he'll never let you be pushed past your limit; he'll always be there to help you come through it."

Esther's two-year-old son, Adam, was diagnosed with a rare, aggressive form of cancer. For two agonizing years, Esther endured with her baby through chemotherapy, hospitalization for amputation of his arm, and futile attempts to assuage his pain before God took Adam home on Valentine's Day. Heartsick, Esther sank into despair and depression to the point of attempting to take her own life.

"When I look back, I see that even as I struggled, Jesus was the One that carried me and gave me life for here and hereafter," Esther says today. "Jesus is the *only* way of escape in terrible situations. As believers, we truly can find strength to overcome and endure trials through the love of Christ."

In times of acute distress, the wheels of everyday life may grind to a screeching, jarring halt. We feel helpless, clueless as to how to lubricate those rusty cogs to set the wheels back in motion and move forward. Based on the experiences of Lauren, Esther, and others who have suffered loss, perhaps those wheels just need a little G-R-E-A-S-E:

G: Grieve. It's okay, dear sister. Mourning is part of the healing process. The pain is deep. Allow yourself to *feel* your loss. The death of a dream can feel as real as the death of a loved one. Denying or ignoring reality only postpones the inevitable. Keep your eyes on Jesus through the grief process; remember, it's His power, His presence that ultimately heals. God really does do broken-heart surgery.

R: Release. Pour out your feelings to Papa God. He understands loss—His beloved Son was ruthlessly beaten and killed. Go ahead, pound on His chest. Scream. Sob. He's a very *big* God. He can take it.

Be assured that crying jags and energy lags are perfectly normal post-crisis release mechanisms. You're in mourning and your body is reacting to your spirit trying to reconcile your loss. You often feel as if you're running on empty and you haven't a clue where or how to refill your tank. Papa God gets it. He owns the pump.

Special note: It's important to set time parameters so healthy release doesn't continue indefinitely and become an unhealthy quagmire of unproductive anger.

E: Establish support. Find a source of regular, ongoing emotional support, such as a group of like-minded, caring women or a trusted friend. People who are safe and understand your vulnerability. Accept their strength to bolster you when yours is gone.

A: Act. Get off that couch, girl. Move your bones. Put one foot in front of the other. Now do it again. Go out. Keep breathing. Keep living. Don't allow yourself to fold up and wither away. You may not *feel* like doing squat, but long-term happiness trumps short-term sacrifice. Remember, healing is a dollar-off coupon, not a blowout sale. It's an incremental process. Step by tiny step, just keep moving in the right direction and eventually you'll get there. You will!

S: Seek godly counsel. Schedule regular sessions with a *Christian* counselor. It's important to get a scriptural perspective during your healing process. You wouldn't ask your hairstylist to fix your car, would you? Of course not—it's not her area of expertise. Your soul is infinitely more important than your carburetor. Seek guidance from a trained representative of your Creator who is entrenched in godly values and spiritual principles.

E: Exercise. Okay, now it's time for some tough self-discipline. Set a specific regular routine not just a vague promise like "I'll climb more steps," but something measurable like "Four flights of stairs each day" or "I'll bike to the park three times every week." Then hold yourself accountable by a checklist.

Walk, run, ski, spin, work out, join the roller derby—whatever waxes your eyebrows, but make it a priority. No weasel words: "*Maybe* I'll go," "*Probably* tomorrow," "*If* it doesn't rain and Jupiter aligns with Mars." Listen, you can't control disasters, but you *can* control whether or not you provide your body the physical outlet it needs to keep your natural chemicals and healing fluids pumping. Do this for *you*.

I believe it's fair to say that 95 percent of us question God's love for us and even His very existence when tragedy strikes. And in our fallen world, it *will* strike everyone at one time or another. My husband, Chuck, and I both went through our own barren desert times in our faith after six heart-wrenching miscarriages. We estranged ourselves from the Lord and wanted nothing more to do with a God who we felt didn't care about us. My desert lasted three lonely years—bad enough—but Chuck's dragged on for a decade.

In the immediate throes of our loss, God seemed cruel and heartless. We felt abandoned and lost, but in retrospect, like Esther, we now see that God was still there all along. Not cruel, not heartless, just silently shining a flashlight of hope and waiting patiently for our self-imposed spiritual cataracts to slough off so we could see His presence.

One of my favorite scriptures of comfort became Psalm 22:24 (look back at the beginning of this chapter). I came to understand that God is not our afflic*tor*; no, He's the helper of the afflic*ted*. That's you and me. He's not the enemy; He's on our team. A huge difference to a healing heart!

Another coping truth recently came to me in my girlcave. (Some call it a kitchen.)

Have you ever baked homemade bread? Nothing smells better this side of heaven! Well, the way I see it, healing is like bread yeast—the dough has to be pulled, stretched, and beat upon to work the yeast throughout, but it finally permeates every inch. Over time, that very yeast enables the bread to rise and become what it was meant to be. If the yeast doesn't pervade the dough, or if the loaf doesn't spend enough time in the oven, the bread will never be completed. It will remain useless, gloppy, inedible dough. Heat is necessary for its transformation and perfection.

So the next time you feel like yelling, "Stick a toothpick in me; I'm done!" remember that although our oven days are difficult—often painful—those are the times we grow and mature in our faith.

*I have learned that pain has purpose, which, at the peak
of excruciating discomfort, brings me little consolation.
Hindsight, though, has often proven pain's value. In fact,
I have found pain to be one of life's most effective teachers.*

PATSY CLAIRMONT

LET'S DECOM-STRESS

1. Describe a recent time when you faced devastating, unexpected loss. How did you deal with it? Are you still dealing with it?

2. Which of the GREASE elements did you implement? Which did you not use? Do you see a need to implement them now?

3. Read Psalm 4 (it's short). How, like David, can we find peace in our distress? What does it mean to be "set apart" (verse 3)?

....

....

....

....

....

....

....

Calendar Constipation
—SIMPLIFY—

"Come to me, all you who are weary
and burdened, and I will give you rest."

MATTHEW 11:28 NIV

I was a young mother, totally ragged out, dragging home from work to fish toys out of the toilet and scrape dog vomit from the rug. I cried out in desperation, "I can't remember the last time I *really* laughed. Am I ever going to feel happy again?"

I came to the cynical conclusion that happiness is merely the absence of pain.

I was frazzled—far too busy, allowing my frantic pace to hijack my happiness and steal my joy. I became chronically weary, trudging through my days, keeping my eyes glued to my to-do list, driven to check off the next item. Never living in the moment but always looking ahead to the time when my schedule would magically slow down and I could finally rest.

But it didn't happen. I continued to take on new projects, worthwhile activities, ministries that needed me. Each worthy task required planning, meetings, creative energy, and time I didn't have. I was always doing this, going there, getting that done.

But do you know what all that *do, do, do* results in? Well, I'm gonna tell you.

It's not something most civilized people discuss (I never let *that* stop me!), but we all know it exists: calendar constipation. Those squares on our calendars are plugged up, choked, clogged. And like any grandpa on Grape-Nuts can tell you, there's only one surefire way to cure calendar constipation: an activities enema.

God doesn't want us to be washed-out dishrags, girlfriend! God is *not* glorified when we are so exhausted that we can't tell we're brushing our hair with a

toothbrush or trying to pay for groceries with our Blockbuster card.

I took a good, hard look at my overloaded schedule and made the decision to scale down, pull back, and simplify. (Love those Wes King lyrics! If you don't know the song "Simplify," pull it up—trust me, you'll wiggle till you giggle!).

An activities enema isn't easy, but really, is anything that's worthwhile? I began to flush out unnecessary activities and wash away anything nonessential to the special ministry God gave me, which at that time was my husband and children.

It took several months of dedicated effort before I found time around the edges of my day. And then gradually, with a little breathing space, I could feel the joy of the Lord again. I started noticing the beauty of sunbeams piercing the early morning mist, dew-touched spiderwebs so much like my grandmother's hand-tatted lace doilies, and slices of kiwi like little smiley faces in my fruit salad.

Beauty was always there; I just couldn't see it when my eyes were focused on my to-do list.

What about you? Are your feet stuck in the muck of everyday stress—that gooey, sticky mud that sucks the energy out of you and pulls you down with such a strong grip, you feel like you'll never escape?

What are some of these *mudsuckers* that keep women bogged down in the swamp of frenzy?

Mudsucker 1: Fatigue. Overextension of our time and energy smothers our inner peace. In his book *The Overload Syndrome*, Dr. Richard Swenson, physician and Christian authority on time management, says, "When we experience a time famine, joy is the first casualty; irritability poisons our attitudes."

Dr. Swenson further states that Christians should pray about new commitments and put them to the litmus test of peace. We should ask ourselves, "Will this commitment result in peace in my heart and my home, or add to the chaos?"

Papa God wants to give us His peace. The devil thrives in chaos.

It helps me to view my daily allotment of energy like a chocolate bar (I relate everything to food!). A gulp here and a nibble there steadily depletes the bar all day long, and once the last bite's gone, it's gone. There's no more. My zip is zapped. I have to learn to ration my energy wisely or I crash and burn w-a-y before the day is done.

Mudsucker 2: Circumstances. My friend Leroy says, "Sometimes it feels like

I've been picked out to be picked on." *Stuff* happens beyond our control and we are forced to deal with it: finances head south, we're miserable at work, health problems blindside us, relationships fail, or family strife fades the color from our world.

But, sister, circumstances don't have to control us. We can't change every situation, but through the Lord's power we can choose our responses to them. And that makes the difference between victory and defeat. "Everyone born of God overcomes the world" (1 John 5:4 NIV). By tapping into Papa God's strength as our own, we choose *not* to allow our circumstances to define us.

Mudsucker 3: People-pleasing. I believe most women have an innate desire to be liked and appreciated by others. We sometimes feel we must take on more and more responsibilities of service to merit that respect and affection. But we must remember: "Our purpose is to please God, not people" (1 Thessalonians 2:4 NLT).

People will greedily take as much of our time and energy as we'll allow them to. God knows our limitations and wants only to benefit us.

Mudsucker 4: Guilt. My dearest beloved spouse says that 90 percent of the reason I ever do anything is guilt. That, of course, is absurd. It's not a smidge over 87. The truth is, many women are unknowingly motivated by guilt: "I really should. . ." "I'll feel terrible if I don't. . ." "I owe it to him/her/them to. . ."

We must learn to differentiate between self-inflicted guilt and God-ordained purpose. One is sin and the other is integrity. Both require precious time, and we must carefully choose how to spend our finite resources of time and energy.

So how can we give our constipated calendars an activities enema?

⁕ Eliminate the nonessentials. Determine your top three priorities—the ministries God has assigned to you at this season of your life. Sit down and study your schedule for the next month. Analyze what motivation is behind each activity: Is it guilt? To please people? Anything other than furthering your God-ordained ministry? Now take a red pen and slash everything not conducive to your priorities. Pick up the phone and explain to those responsible that you are sorry but you must scale back to maintain your mental and spiritual health and cannot participate at this time. No one can argue with that reasoning. They're afraid they'll contribute to sending you to either the loony bin or jail.

- Repeat this process the following month. Ruthlessly trim the fat. Stick to your resolve to deactivate those mudsuckers.
- Communicate with Papa God every day in every way. Pray as if your life depends on it—because it does! Grasp those fleeting opportunities to recognize God's fingerprints in the details of your everyday life.
- Read the instructions. Make a plan and stick to it in reading and studying God's Word daily. This is how we replenish our depleted reserves.
- Simplify, yes, but preserve the important stuff. Keep a list of your top three priorities taped to your mirror. Schedule time with the people in your life who matter most: your husband, your children, and *you*, girl.

Writers have a cardinal rule when penning a novel: protect the white space. You know, the blank part of the paper not covered with black letters. White space makes the page appear more reader-friendly. White space feels nonintimidating, conquerable, even inviting.

White space is important in de-cluttering our lives, too.

Remember how it felt to wake up on a gloriously free summer morning when you were a kid? Ah, the exultation of knowing you had empty hours to fill any way you liked!

As adults, we don't often have the luxury of having free hours, but we can carve free minutes out of each day if we diligently simplify and unclog those constipated calendars. That, dear sister, is when we reconnect with that summer morning feeling. The joy of the Lord brings splashes of color back into our black-and-white world.

There's never enough time to do all the nothing you want.

BILL WATTERSON, *CALVIN AND HOBBES*

LET'S DECOM-STRESS

1. Are you suffering from calendar constipation? Are you in need of an activities enema? So what are you going to do about it, girl?

2. Which mudsuckers do you struggle with most?

3. Stop a minute and create a workable plan for introducing a little more white space into your day. Enlist your family members' help;they can be your strongest allies.

As You Wish
—Intentional Submission—

Do nothing from selfishness or empty conceit, but with humility of mind regard one another as more important than yourselves.

Philippians 2:3 nasb

"Because I'm the manager, and I'll do whatever I want!"

It was the third time within three weeks I'd heard that phrase from my new boss, Lorna. I felt like I was back on the second-grade playground and we were haggling over a jump rope.

This time it was Lorna's response to my question of why she had discarded supplies (without asking) that I regularly used for my patients. Last time it was in reference to her hanging the clinic wall clock where it was visible from everywhere but my work area. Before that, it accompanied her refusal to provide an extra chair so I didn't have to keep moving my one assigned chair around.

Little things in the grand scheme of work life, maybe, but important to me.

Lord, what have I gotten myself into? It was the gazillionth time I'd flung that question heavenward since transferring to this rehabilitation clinic. I was having a hard time maintaining a professional demeanor with my new supervisor who was blunt, headstrong, micromanaging, and twenty years my junior.

What I really wanted was to set her panties on fire.

Since I'd arrived, my requests for standard supplies had been ignored. I didn't think they were unreasonable—a stapler, a tape dispenser, a file cabinet for my home-exercise handouts.

Why, oh why am I here, Lord? Yet my decision to transfer had been made after

weeks of earnest prayer. Sure, I'd heard rumors about Lorna's control issues, but I couldn't get past the nagging feeling that God wanted me here. And now I wondered if I had jumped from the proverbial frying pan into the Hades Misery Manufacturing Plant.

During my fourth week trekking across the clinic to the office every time I needed the only stapler on the premises, the administrative assistant whispered, "I don't know why she won't let me order you a stapler. It's a ridiculous power play to prove she's in charge."

With a quick glance to assure Lorna was out of earshot, she continued, "If it was me, I'd bring a stapler from home. . .and a good pair of earplugs."

If she only knew how many times I had considered just that. A stapler rode shotgun in my purse nearly every morning, but something always made me return it to my kitchen drawer before leaving the house. I knew if I brought my own, Lorna would go ballistic, but that wasn't really what stopped me.

I'm ashamed to admit that I've experienced my share of shredding insufferable tyrants with my cat-o'-nine-tails tongue. Nope, I'm not usually shy about sticking up for my "rights" (as I selfishly perceive them, of course), but somehow I knew this time God wanted me to put a sock in it.

Lest you erroneously think I'm a vestige of holiness, holding back was absolute torture for me. I prayed daily to have not only my Father's eyes but His teeth to clamp down on my rogue tongue. And true to His word, He provided supernatural grace for me *not* to explode with searing righteous anger when I thought I was being treated unfairly.

It was a strange, almost out-of-body experience: watching myself react calmly—as if I actually *were* spiritually mature and self-controlled when deep down, I seethed with burning, sometimes consuming rage. But overriding that rage was my complete dependency on God for the power to intentionally submit to Lorna despite my anger.

Intentionally submit. Defer. Not cave in because of weakness but willingly yield to her leadership from a position of strength. Give her permission to lead and, more importantly, give myself permission to follow.

Not a natural inclination; no, I'm not that righteous. A deliberate decision. It was as if God were saying, "Dig deep, Deb. A soul is at stake here. Let her win the battles; I'll win the war."

Then one day, in a rare vulnerable moment, Lorna smiled. It was a genuine smile, not the faux model I'd come to expect. Something intangible shifted between us. Words began to flow. She spoke of her childhood as the youngest of eight children who felt she was never allowed to control her own life or display her capabilities. Then as an adult she'd never had much need for a God who might stifle her freedom. And if she didn't maintain rigid control, she feared the seams of her life might begin unraveling and never stop.

Wow. She seemed so, well. . .human. Not at all like the steel-skinned, fire-breathing monster I had built up in my mind. I began to notice her good qualities: generosity (she brought us souvenirs from her European vacation), her willingness to bail me out of my frequent computer messes, and the broad scope of her technical knowledge. Why couldn't I appreciate those before? Hmm.

I realized that because I had forfeited the skirmishes, she felt comfortable enough in my (perceived) respect for her to risk opening up. I thanked God that He'd kept my tongue tied.

The following week, I arrived at work to find a stapler and tape dispenser sitting on my desk. Soon a clock appeared on the wall across from my treatment table and an extra chair eventually found its way to my area. And best of all, Lorna was tolerant of me speaking about my best friend, Jesus.

Everything wasn't exactly happily ever after between us, but my eyes were opened to the Lord's covert wisdom in nudging me toward intentional submission and *not* inflaming the situation while He worked on Lorna's heart concerning things about which I couldn't possibly have known. "GOD, our God, will take care of the hidden things" (Deuteronomy 29:29 MSG).

You know what I learned? Submitting to others boils down to a matter of trust that the Lord is in ultimate control.

When we choose to submit to someone in authority over us, we're actually submitting to God. If He truly *is* in control, He orchestrates the channels of authority in which we live, work, and function. As believers, our ultimate goal is to become Christlike, and Christ exemplified willing submission to His Father by humbling Himself even to the point of death.

Remember the scene from the classic movie *The Princess Bride* (one of my

all-time faves!) when Buttercup shoves her masked rescuer down the steep hill overlooking the fire swamp and suddenly realizes that he's none other than her "sweet Wesley," her thought-to-be-deceased true love? Instead of trying to save himself as he tumbles for what seems an eternity, Wesley's simple words of submission, "As you wish," linger in his wake.

He's willing to take the fall if that's what love requires of him.

May "as you wish" be our love-motivated creed, too, as we submit to Philippians 2:3 and humble ourselves to the point of viewing others as more important than ourselves.

> True strength lies in submission,
> which permits one to dedicate his life,
> through devotion, to something beyond himself.
>
> HENRY MILLER

LET'S DECOM-STRESS

1. So whose panties do you want to set on fire?

2. Do you have difficulty with intentional submission? Describe your last skirmish. Who won the battle? Who's winning the war?

3. What "hidden things" might God be addressing through this relationship?

Gray: The New Blond
—WORRY—

*"Who of you by worrying can add
a single hour to your life? Since you
cannot do this very little thing,
why do you worry about the rest?"*

LUKE 12:25–26 NIV

When I hear women my age grouse about discovering new gray hairs reflected
in the mirror each morning, I simply smile serenely and say, "Ah, 'tis but a trivial
matter to me. I shall never turn gray."

At this point they either turn to me with a question mark or a machete in their
eyes and respond, "How can you be so sure?"

"Very simple, really," I acquiesce with grace and assurance, patting my golden
locks. "I pay good money to be a natural blond."

The only trouble is that my faux blond (gray incognito) sprigs are wiry and
frizzy, and unless I spend precious time flattening them out like *real* hairs, I end
up looking like a yellow Chia Pet. I really can't comprehend why a compassionate
God allows hormones to do such a nasty number on hair as we age. Why does
gray hair have to sprout like bread wrapper twist ties? Isn't it bad enough that our
other bodily assets are either traveling south or expanding like pasta in a soup pot?

Worrying about the advancing armies of salt infiltrating our pepper is
counterproductive. It only perpetuates the problem and results in an even stronger
resemblance to Marie Antoinette. Or Steve Martin. Or, in my case, Don King.

Besides, there are far too many other things to worry about. And I should
know; I latch onto vexation like a gator on a goose. Over the years I have honed
the art of worry into a science. I've systematically and diligently transformed

molehills into mountains. I've whipped pesky irritants into frothy, acetic colon-coaters and fretted over annoying burdens until they invaded my dreams.

But I've come to realize Jesus was absolutely right in the passage at the beginning of this chapter (big *duh*—isn't He always right?). I love *The Message* translation: "Has anyone by fussing before the mirror ever gotten taller by so much as an inch? If fussing can't even do that, why fuss at all?"

I mean really, what's all the fuss about?

It's actually a form of self-centeredness: Fussing, worrying, obsessing. . .simply keeps us focused on *getting* instead of *giving*. We somehow think by stewing about a problem we'll suddenly gain insight into how to manipulate circumstances to make something miraculous happen. As if our preoccupation can somehow move the hand of God and shift things toward our desired result.

Maybe we should just turn in our application for Queen of the Universe and be done with it. If we were in charge, at least we wouldn't be hocking up our agitations over and over like a Guernsey regurgitating her cud. We would know what to do. In the words of Terri Guillemets, "You can never worry your way to enlightenment."

Worry can change us in intangible ways: negative, personality-altering ways. Our joy drains away like water in an unplugged sink, and hope is replaced by angst and dread.

We may begin to talk too much (combativeness) or too little (withdrawal). We lose touch with today and instead dwell on regretting yesterday or changing tomorrow.

As a result, we feel listless, spent. We may also experience stress-induced pain or aching in organs, muscles, or joints. Many systemic diseases like fibromyalgia, multiple sclerosis, or lupus are believed to be exacerbated by worry, stress, fatigue, or an imbalanced lifestyle.

Amid worry, our listening skills deteriorate, too. We can't hear our own bodies crying out for attention. We bury twinges, jitters, and migraines with pills, antacids, caffeine, or my sedative of choice, chocolate. We don't hear others well either. Our God-given feminine sensitivity becomes debilitated when we're bone-weary and miss what's beneath the words. We tend to jump to erroneous conclusions, often imagining the worst of people.

For example, instead of picking up an unspoken plea for compassion beneath the request of a neighbor who asks if you could drop her son off at school, you immediately decide that she's a selfish egoist who hasn't a clue how overstrained your schedule already is. You bristle instead of sympathize. Consequently, you either resent or avoid her. Your relationship may be irreparably damaged when, in truth, you would help in a flash if you knew her marriage is crumbling and she'll lose her job if she's late again.

When we chronically worry, we don't see what's *really* happening; truth is obscured by lies we choose to believe. It's okay. Everything's fine. Sure, I'm exhausted and miserable right now but it'll be better next week. Next month. Next year.

Sister, it's time to do something about being a worry slave *today.*

How can we turn off that oppressive fret faucet? The first step is to give your worries to Jesus. When your hands start wringing or the mental obsession recorder hits REPLAY for the tenth time, lay your problems at the foot of the cross. Jesus will take them off your hands. Repeat this process every time you try to wrestle them back.

Next, change channels. Distraction is your friend. When I find my guts beginning to churn, I take a prayer walk or bike ride to change the scenery and snag a mental breath of fresh air. Some find peace by digging for it in the garden. Others immerse themselves in cooking or dancing or art. Even—hard for me to believe—housework. My friend Lisa cranks up the praise music and grabs the vacuum. Positive input reduces negative output. You can't bite your nails while scrubbing the linoleum.

Losing yourself in music is a great way to let go of niggling worries. Research has concluded that music can induce positive changes in blood pressure, body temperature, heart and respiration rates, and, most importantly, the hormones produced by stress. Chilling to your favorite music can definitely have a calming, healing effect on frayed nerves. So why not stop right now and collect your preferred CDs or tapes for the car, office, or living room? Wherever their magical musical-relaxing fingers are needed to massage most, keep them handy.

Writing down your concerns is an effective tool for breaking the worry cycle. Journaling is cathartic on many levels. It really does relieve stress and give you a solid approach for resolving problems rather than stewing in them. Not only does

writing about your frustrations enable you to express the emotions you're not comfortable verbalizing, it often helps you organize your thoughts to better help you deal with them. And your journal can serve as a springboard for keeping track of prayer requests and monitoring God's loving responses.

I heard about a minister who instructed members of his congregation to jot down all their worries and store them a shoe box on their top closet shelf. They were not allowed to look at them until the end of the month. By the second week, people began forgetting all about them. By the fourth week, many things had resolved themselves and were no longer an issue.

"Be anxious for nothing" (Philippians 4:6 NASB) takes on new meaning when you grasp the fact that anxiety does absolutely nothing for you.

Every evening I turn my worries over to God.
He's going to be up all night anyway.
MARY C. CROWLEY

LET'S DECOM-STRESS

1. Think back a moment: What were your top three worries this time last year? You're above average if you can remember more than one. What does that tell you about the transient nature of worrying?

2. Mark Twain said, "Drag your thoughts away from your troubles. . . by the ears, by the heels, or any other way you can manage it." Brainstorm three practical ways you can distance yourself from worrying.

3. Read Isaiah 46:4. How does God's reassurance that He'll take care of you when you have snow on your roof affect the way you live today?

Striving for a Low-Strife Life
—FAMILY ORGANIZATION—

*For God is not a God of disorder
but of peace.*

1 CORINTHIANS 14:33 NIV

Kate plus eight has nothing on my friend Tammy. Mother of eleven children, including one severely disabled son requiring 24-7 care, Tammy and her husband, Scott, a communications company project manager, raised their first nine children in a four-bedroom, two-bath home in a tidy subdivision where the average family numbered four.

In 2002, God blessed them with a 3,000-square-foot home they built on twelve acres of rolling pastureland. Grazing cows dot the green expanse along the winding dirt road climbing the hill to the two-story frame house with a wide, welcoming front porch.

It takes extraordinary organization to keep from imploding with one girl and seven lively boys between the ages of four and fifteen—all homeschooled—still in residence. A computerized spreadsheet of chores covers the refrigerator door, along with a star chart offering positive incentives to keep the kids on track with their individual responsibilities. Chores include caring for the two family dogs, cows, sheep, and chickens.

Everyone in this house helps with laundry, dishes, cooking, and cleaning. A ten-foot, picnic-bench-style kitchen table is set, plates are stacked, cups are color coded, and dishes are washed three times daily. Tammy rotates the chore list corresponding to the skills, preferences, and needs of her offspring.

For instance, Samuel, the thirteen-year-old, likes to cook and is becoming quite an accomplished chef, but tends to be a little *untidy* with food preparation.

So Tammy rotates him to kitchen cleanup so he'll become more aware of the repercussions of messiness. This is not trivial stuff. She knows he's establishing lifelong habits.

Locking her gentle gaze on his green eyes, she succinctly defines the reasons for the task order: "First clean the counters and appliances so loose pieces fall to the floor. Then clear large or gooey floor debris before sweeping so the broom doesn't stick. Mop last, but only after your brothers have evacuated the kitchen, or all previous steps will have to be repeated."

She smiles encouragingly. "Got it?"

He nods and gets to work. Tammy has just taught a man to fish for a lifetime instead of forking over the catch of the day. You can bet his future wife will be thrilled.

After twenty-three years of trial and error, Tammy states that her parenting style is more *discipling* than *disciplining*. Being consistent, walking through problems calmly, and taking time to explain the reasons for expected behavior enable her to maintain order and focus on the spiritual dimension in every aspect of the family's life. "Strife may be considered normal," she concedes, tucking a stray auburn tendril behind her ear, "but it's not godly."

So how does a mother of eleven handle stress?

"Oh, I've tried yelling," she admits readily, "but it does no good. The key is recognizing you can't do it in your own strength. Then you're totally dependent on God's grace, and He never lets you down."

To keep her own grace reserves from draining dry, Tammy makes spending daily time with her Lord a priority. She and Scott arise at six o'clock to the titillating invitation of the coffeemaker and small refrigerator tucked into the corner of their bedroom. They enjoy a private hour of Bible reading, chatting, and praying together before the kids rise at seven. "They know this is our special time and they're not allowed to interrupt. We encourage them to read their Bibles and pray, too, before they come down for breakfast at 7:30."

Besides chores and a mandatory hour of outside playtime in the morning and afternoon, the average day is spent poring over books, projects, and schoolwork in one of the rambling home's ten bedrooms, which is designated as the classroom. The younger kids work amid map-covered walls and well-stocked bookshelves, while the older boys spread out at the supersized kitchen table.

Free time produces games, puzzles, and imaginative toys, including incredibly intricate Lego creations. TV is watched only sporadically, and computer games are reserved for Saturdays. Family camping trips are a highly anticipated treat.

"I absolutely love homeschooling," Tammy says, her soft voice resonating with passion. "After experiencing public and private education with my older children, I'll never do anything else. I love teaching my kids from a biblical worldview. We want to focus on these foundational developmental years and prepare them to launch into the world for Christ.

"I think it's important for parents to know what's going in and what's going out of their children's lives. If we don't"—as she pauses her eyes drift downward, hinting at an invisible wound from somewhere in her past—"we may lose them to the world."

Scott takes the father's biblical mandate of spiritual leadership seriously. He leads a nightly family devotional, which includes robust singing, scripture reading, discussion, and prayer. For variety, sometimes scriptural training videos or faith-based audio messages are included.

What about "me" time?

Tammy shrugs. "After everything else gets done. Makeup's last, as you can see." She grins, bare-faced. "Scott and I have just begun biking together daily, and we try to have a date night once a week. The older boys watch the little ones, and we escape to talk about goals and dreams and laugh over war stories from the foxholes of our crazy life."

Tammy pursues daily face time with each of her children, although with a family this large, sharing Mom's time—as well as space and belongings—with siblings is a process. "Learning to show love and patience to each other is a necessary way of life in our family," Tammy says as small heads all around her bob in agreement.

Family life has long revolved around fifteen-year-old Caleb, unable to speak or care for himself since birth. Multiple hospitalizations for painful medical procedures required separation from the family, sometimes for many weeks, when Tammy or Scott—or both—never left his side. The other children stepped up to take on greater responsibility for themselves and their siblings through the hard times during which they almost lost Caleb.

Tammy recalls a pivotal "Abraham moment" that brought the entire family to its knees. Physicians gave no hope for Caleb. "We were devastated, but decided to let him go and release him completely to God. We felt like Abraham must have felt when he faced the possibility of burying his son [see Genesis 22], but still he chose to trust God, whatever the outcome."

Tammy's eyes sparkle when she recalls the neurosurgeon's description of Caleb's recovery: "Divine intervention."

Scott and Tammy believe growing up with a special-needs brother has taught Caleb's siblings compassion, belief in miracles, and, most importantly,the truth that no matter what condition you're in, you can always lead people to Christ. Seven nurses have committed their lives to Christ while working with Caleb. Twelve-year-old Gabe sums up the family's attitude best: "A little bit of difficulty doesn't make it *hard*."

So what applicable organizational take-aways can we glean from this remarkable family?

- Establish a plan. Running any household by the seat of your pants produces only chaos and frustration.
- Make daily time with Papa God a priority. Tight schedules are no excuse. If it's important to you, you'll find a way to carve out time.
- No matter how organized you are, something will eventually go awry. Don't freak. Expect it. Take control of your attitude so that your attitude doesn't take control of you. Repeat Gabe's motto: "A little bit of difficulty doesn't make it *hard*."
- Consistently refresh your reserves—your level of dependency on God's grace and patience is reflected in your grace and patience toward others.

> I have not failed. I've just found
> ten thousand ways that won't work.
>
> THOMAS EDISON

LET'S DECOM-STRESS

1. Tammy is an ordinary woman with an extraordinary attitude. What organizational tips can you borrow to apply to your family?

2. How do you think a household of ten manages to have a daily family worship time despite "a little bit of difficulty"?

3. How do you replenish your family's faith reserves on a daily basis?

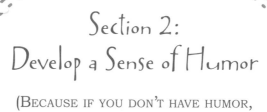

Section 2:
Develop a Sense of Humor

(BECAUSE IF YOU DON'T HAVE HUMOR,
YOU PROBABLY DON'T HAVE MUCH SENSE!)

DEFEATING THE JOY-SUCKING DULLY-FUNKS

*I haven't trusted polls since I read that 62
percent of women had affairs during their
lunch hour. I've never met a woman in my
life who would give up lunch for sex.*
ERMA BOMBECK

The Back Forty: Years, Not Acres
—Becoming a Packing Granny—

*I will still be the same when you are
old and gray, and I will take care of you.*

Isaiah 46:4 CEV

I love the story about the grandmother who exited a grocery store to find four men piling into her car. The men fled when she pulled a pistol from her purse and waved it in the air, screaming, "I have a gun, and I know how to use it!"

While loading her groceries into the backseat, the woman noticed a football, a Frisbee, and two six-packs of beer. She then spied her car parked four spaces away.

Big oops.

When she arrived at the police station to report her mistake, she encountered four pale men reporting a carjacking by a mad elderly woman, less than five feet tall, glasses, curly white hair, packing a large handgun.

Bette Davis was right: "Old age ain't no place for sissies."

Hey, we don't have to pack guns to become a packing granny. It's *attitude* that's our secret weapon as we explore the back forty. The back forty? You know, those mysterious years on the other side of the hill.

The far side of the hill creeps up on you when you're still panting and sweaty from clawing up the front side. At the hill's peak, you pass that midcentury mark in age; the kids are grown, people and jobs and responsibilities aren't pulling you in a thousand directions at once (quite as much as before), and you have the tiniest bit of space to rediscover *you*. You take a deep breath, smile, and cuddle up with a good book and a triple mocha latte.

Suddenly, the ground falls out from under you and you're skidding down the back slope of the hill. Hormones disappear, long-lost pounds reappear, memory disintegrates, and the face staring back at you from the mirror looks alarmingly like your great-aunt Hilda's.

Wrinkles form in the dead of night. You know, if I listen closely, I can hear my flesh creasing and crinkling when I pad to the bathroom in the wee hours. (It must've been a woman who coined the phrase *wee hours* on a midnight potty run.) The creation of the world probably sounded like this, as God enthusiastically gouged rivers and trenches and valleys from the smooth, blemish-free earth.

That reminds me of the night after I wallpapered my daughter's nursery without sufficient paste. The poor baby kept waking up, screaming, and as I sat in the rocker nursing her at 4:00 a.m., I discovered why. The strangest rustling noises surrounded us from all sides of the room, totally creepy. It sounded like enormous snakes slithering behind the walls. It turned out that by morning, every single sheet of wallpaper had slowly peeled off the wall, crackling in protest until crumpling to the floor in a wilted wad of disgrace.

Too bad the sheets of facial wrinkles won't follow suit.

Once those wrinkles (hey, I prefer to think of them as smile footprints) are set into the fabric of our being, there's no good way to iron them out (shy of a surgical tuck). My bulging shelf of antiwrinkle cream and firming eye ointment attests to that!

And heaven forbid your aim is off when applying your mascara—erasing an errant smudge in that putty skin beneath the eye is like trying to wipe blueberry sauce off runny cheesecake. It just goos and smears worse than ever. The older I get, the more I resemble a grease-painted quarterback ready for the big game. Can't even scrawl in a Bible verse like my football hero, Tim Tebow. (I graduated in the University of Florida's class of '79; gooooo Gators! *Obnoxious alligator chomp here.*)

There must be a way to use gravity to our advantage. Maybe ditching our bras would pull the wrinkles out of our faces. But then we'd have to tuck our bosoms into our knee-highs to keep from tripping over them.

Some gals put the skids on the downhill descent by running back up the hill. Like the sixty-six-year-old Spanish woman who had her uterus rejuvenated with hormone therapy and gave birth to twins after she'd been in menopause for eighteen years. No kidding.

Ay yi yi. Can you imagine confusing the baby's vitamins with your Geritol? Or preparing his juice bottle while slurping your morning Metamucil? Or watching him cut new teeth while yours are soaking in a glass of Efferdent?

Well, Sarah was ninety when God granted her heart's desire and she gave birth to Isaac (see Genesis 21). I'll bet she never once complained about trading her wheelchair for a baby stroller.

After all, God's in the miracle business, and He "*is* able to do far more abundantly beyond all that we ask or think, according to the power that works within us" (Ephesians 3:20 NASB, emphasis mine). That power, of course, is His enormous, undefeatable power.

Don't you love the promise in those exciting words and phrases—*far more*, *abundantly*, and *beyond*? There's hope for us, sisters! You and I *can* be Cinderella! Through Papa God's power working within us, we can transform into a new, improved version of ourselves beyond our most extravagant imaginings.

I'm living proof that age is only a number. I began writing at age forty-five when my youngest chick flew the coop. While sitting in a dentist's office, praying about what to do with my life, I heard God's still, small voice whisper that it was finally time to pursue my lifelong dream of becoming a writer. Now eight years, one hundred articles, and thirteen books later, my heart bursts with His blessings *far more*, *abundantly*, *beyond* my wildest dreams.

It's never too late to become a packing granny as long as we harbor attitudes of expectation, wonder, and excitement about what's around the next twist in the road! What back-forty harvest does Papa God have in store for you?

She's no chicken; she's on the
wrong side of thirty, if she be a day.
JONATHAN SWIFT, *GULLIVER'S TRAVELS*

LET'S DECOM-STRESS

1. What do you picture yourself doing at age sixty? How about eighty?

2. If your life continues on its current track, what things might you one day wish you had done? What gifts and abilities will you regret not pursuing?

3. Name two areas of your life in which God has blessed you "far more abundantly beyond" your expectations. As we tread water in the stress-pool of life, we may not always *feel* blessed, but we definitely *are* blessed. Thank Him for His loving-kindness and provision.

The Ever-Laughing Life
—Humor in the Trenches—

*If we are "out of our mind,"
as some say, it is for God.*
2 Corinthians 5:13 NIV

The crisp linen tablecloths and sparkling china at the country club luncheon made me feel like a regal princess. Having been invited to speak to the Society of Artsy-Smartsy Women (name changed to protect the uppity) was a thrill for me. I don't dine outside McDonald's much.

I dabbed the corners of my mouth with my white cloth napkin as a starched waiter hovered nearby to refill my iced tea goblet. The dainty chicken salad croissant and bowl of creamy clam chowder I'd been served had my full attention.

The newspaper reporter across the table asked about the release date of my upcoming book, and the acclaimed artist sitting beside her chimed in with her own question. Both meticulously made-up and coiffed ladies gazed serenely at me, waiting patiently while I attempted to dispose of the spoonful of clam chowder in my mouth.

But something was amiss. The potato cubes disappeared cooperatively down the ole gullet, but a large rubbery clam, too big to swallow whole and too gristly to masticate properly, kept bouncing between my teeth like a pinball.

What to do? Choke down the glob and risk getting to know my new society friends intimately through a Heimlich hug? Not an option. The good ladies were waiting.

Smiling inanely, I just kept chewing. I chewed and chewed and chewed. That clam was like bubblegum with superpowers. The reporter began to look bored and the artist raised her perfectly arched left eyebrow as if pondering a deep philosophical point. Finally, as they cast perplexed glances at one another, I seized the opportunity to spit the rebellious bolus into my napkin.

The wad of seafood felt warm in my palm as I gripped it securely through the cloth in my lap. All was well as I conversed with my neighbors until the waiter reappeared and extended a platter of luscious chocolate cheesecake in my general direction.

Without a second thought (my usual reaction to dessert), I reached for the dish with both hands and, in doing so, relinquished my grip on the prisoner. Out of my balled-up napkin tumbled that chewed-up chunk of chowder, plopping right atop the purse hanging on the chair in back of the woman beside me.

It was Gucci.

The only witness was the poker-faced waiter who straightened, inhaled sharply, turned, and retreated to the kitchen, undoubtedly to entertain the chef with his you-won't-believe-this story. My frantic mind raced. I had to get rid of that nasty shellfish!

Providentially, one of the ladies was regaling my elegant tablemates with an amusing story. As polite laughter tittered in response, I swept my arms outward in a gesture of unfettered glee, strategically swatting that disgusting wad of food beneath the table. But my aim was a smidge high. The confounded thing rebounded against the draped tablecloth and bounced to a rolling stop on the plush carpet just behind my chair.

My breathing grew shallow. A heat wave encompassed me. *Think, Debbie!*

Horrified, I quietly excused myself to go to the restroom, wondering if I might feign a loose shoelace in order to bend over and remove the evidence of my crime. I glanced at my feet. No good. I was wearing pumps.

As I stood and turned to face my humiliating destiny, a potted ficus in the corner about six feet away caught my eye. Thank you, Lord! You *do* provide for Your children in need. Without a moment's hesitation, I took a running step toward the gnawed clam and, using my best soccer stroke, kicked a line drive straight and true behind the ceramic ficus vase. Glancing quickly around, I saw no apparent witnesses. Everyone was focused on their cheesecake.

Heaving a sigh of relief, I beat a retreat toward the ladies' room, breathing easier with every step. As I passed the swinging door to the kitchen, the waiter

solemnly stepped out. Staring straight ahead and without cracking the slightest smile, he muttered, "Goal," before glancing my way with a telltale wink.

Humor is important. It's a catalyst for releasing God's rejuvenating joy into our souls. Humor is God's weapon against worry, anxiety, and fear. It's a powerful salve for the skinned knees of the spirit. . .healing, revitalizing, protecting us against toxic infections like bitterness, defeat, or depression.

Laughter is our lifeline when we're sinking into the pit of rigidity, when we're so absorbed in the stressful details of our lives that we're missing the fun. The sun hasn't disappeared just because it's temporarily obscured by clouds. Sometimes those silver linings are just a belly laugh away.

*If you can't make it better,
you can laugh at it.*

Erma Bombeck

Let's Decom-stress

1. What was your most embarrassing (recent) moment? Is it funny yet? Sometimes it takes a little time to see the humor in a mortifying situation. Imagine seeing your situation through the eyes of Robin Williams, Chonda Pierce, or Patsy Clairmont. How would one of them describe it?

2. What makes you laugh? Your roly-poly puppy? Funny movies? A favorite comedian? So when was the last time you set yourself up for a good belly laugh?

3. Why not kick seriousness out for the evening and plan a night of hysteria? Include the people and things (foods, games, movies, goofy clothes) that make you smile and indulge in a little hilarity. I'll bet your stress level will drop five floors!

Chocolate Makes My Jeans Shrink
—FOOD CHOICES—

When you have eaten and are satisfied,
praise the LORD your God
for the good land he has given you.
DEUTERONOMY 8:10 NIV

Okay. My soul's had enough chicken soup, thank you. Now it needs a little stimulation; you know—a choc-tastic attitude adjustment, mocha milkshake for the mind, chinning up with chocolate chunks.

When writing my book *Mom NEEDS Chocolate*, my mantra was "God, Godiva, and girlfriends—what more do we need?" I was amazed at the multitude of women with whom that simple theme resonated. Apparently we're a society of secret choco-sisters. And some of us are not so secret.

During a weeklong girls' getaway with my friend Cheryl, we visited a quaint, mountainside white-steepled church one Sunday morning. In a stroke of outstanding fortune, I discovered a dark chocolate–coated mint in my purse just as we drove up. And it was only about three months old. "Thank You, Lord!" I nearly shouted, scraping off most of the lint and popping the sweet treat into my mouth as we strode into the church.

(Incidentally, for me chocolate is a medical necessity. I suffer from CDD, chocolate deficit disorder, so my proper medication dosage—a choco-infusion every few hours—is very important for my temperament stability and the mental health of those around me. You might consider this diagnosis for yourself.)

As Cheryl and I greeted our way through the lobby, extended hands and broad smiles showered us from all sides. Returning the friendly smiles of the church folk, I noticed that many released my hand a mite quicker than usual and a

few suddenly found their shoes extremely interesting.

I followed Cheryl into a pew just as the piano prelude began. Turning to ask me a question, her eyes rounded to dinner plates as the grin froze on her horrified face.

"Deb, are you chewing tobacco?"

"What?"

"Your teeth are black. You look. . .um, scary."

Oh no! I slapped a hand over my mouth. The dark chocolate must've infiltrated my "invisible" braces. The only way to get the stain out was to scrub the denture-like clear plastic plates with a toothbrush.

As the congregation rose to its feet for the first praise song, I asked the lady beside me for directions to the restroom, discreetly keeping my hand over my lower face as if I were scratching my nose. She pointed to a door in the very front of the church just to the right of the pulpit. Merciful heavens. I'd have to march up the aisle right past the praise leader boisterously waving his arms and practically climb over the minister whose chair blocked the door.

At that precise moment, the praise leader boomed out instructions for the members to meet and greet their esteemed visitors during the next verse. He nodded regally to Cheryl and me as if we were visiting royalty.

Mortified, I pasted on a closed-lip grin and nodded my head, like a bobble-head doll on a dashboard, to dozens of smiling faces. As soon as heads bowed for the first prayer, I popped out my chocolate-smeared plates, spit on the underside hem of my blouse and rubbed ferociously. That worked fairly well except for the deepest cracks between the molded-plastic teeth. My bicuspids looked as if they were outlined with a black Sharpie. Or as if I were a happy motorcyclist who had just navigated a swarm of flies.

So much for dignity.

Did you know that the average American consumes 11.7 pounds of chocolate each year? That's roughly the weight of a lawn chair! Why, if not for chocolate, there would be little need for stretch denim. Or control panels. Or female subterfuge.

I mean, really, which of us hasn't stashed Tootsie Rolls among the potted plants? Or hidden M&M's in her ibuprofen bottle? Or buried telltale Snickers wrappers inside balled-up paper towels in the trash can?

A friend with a secret choco-addiction once confided that her bamboozled husband, after taking out the garbage, couldn't fathom why there were empty chocolate icing cans at the bottom of every trash can in the house. He couldn't remember eating even one cake!

I saw a wonderful definition of feminine might on a plaque: "True strength is breaking a chocolate bar into four pieces bare-handed. . .and then eating only one."

Of course there are the health issues of chocolate consumption to consider. I certainly don't plan to condemn myself to an early grave because I selfishly refuse to sacrificially down my daily Dove bar. Why, look at Peggy Griffith of Abbotsham, UK. This feisty one-hundred-year-old claims she's eaten thirty chocolate bars per week (that's approximately four *each day*) for over ninety years, which translates to over 14,000 pounds of chocolate.

This granny's got game!

Ironically, while recently driving to my local candy shop, I heard on the radio that scientists had discovered a natural extract in chocolate that cleans teeth better than toothpaste. Hey, I'll bite!

Now if you think about it statistically (as you know, I'm the queen of near-facts of science), it makes zero sense to say no-no to cocoa when you consider that a chocolate bar contains about 500 calories. At just one per day, that's 3,500 calories per week, which roughly equals one pound of body weight—an intake of 156 pounds over a three-year period. For the average 140-pound woman, that means that without chocolate, she would have disappeared six months ago.

See—our very lives depend upon chocolate!

Even researchers at Johns Hopkins University attest to the medical benefits of chocolate. They found that flavanol in dark chocolate thins the blood and helps prevent heart attack and stroke just like aspirin. One small caveat, however: to match the effects of a daily baby aspirin, the dosage would have to be two chocolate bars. That's 1,000 extra calories *each day.*

Hmm. A food exchange could even it out. For health's sake, I for one would be willing to sacrifice green, red, and yellow foods to accommodate the extra brown food intake. It's not my fault they happen to be vegetables. You know, if physicians implemented this protocol, chocolate treatment compliance would be

outstanding, but annoying side effects may include having to wear dentures and getting our bodies wedged between parked cars.

We *can* indulge in that delightful, creamy, delicious stuff, but we must strike a balance. A balance in our nutrition, our diets, and our greed for more.

This theory was reinforced as I recently checked out of the grocery store. The elderly woman in front of me, purchasing a jug of milk, a dozen eggs, and a loaf of bread, sized up my stack of Lean Cuisines topped with three gigantic Cadbury bars. Her wrinkled face suddenly lit up with a coy grin. As she reached for a Hershey bar on the candy rack, she confided with a knowing wink, "Life's all about *balance*, isn't it, dear?"

Avoid any diet that discourages the use of hot fudge.

DON KARDONG

LET'S DECOM-STRESS

1. Have you ever been busted for a secret vice? How did you deal with it?

2. Read Ecclesiastes 5:18. What does Solomon, the wisest man who ever lived, believe is the best way to live our short lives?

3. How do you find balance in your culinary adventures?

Cobwebs in My Mop Bucket
—MANAGING MESSINESS—

*"First clean the inside of
the cup and dish, and then
the outside also will be clean."*
MATTHEW 23:26 NIV

In the Deep South, pests (including children) are a constant stress-producer. Between dismembered lizard tails (often still wiggling), spiderweb hairnets (better on top of the head than walking into one face-first), and separating the pepper from the roach eggs, the animal kingdom that is our home wages a full-time battle.

In fact, German cockroaches are more common in Florida homes than suntans. Those little irritants have developed resistance to insecticides and not only refuse to ingest poisoned bait but pass the immunity gene on to their offspring (a single female can produce thousands in a year).

How about some other fun roach facts to ruminate upon in bed tonight? (If you're bug-squeamish, skip to the next paragraph.) Did you know a roach can live up to a week without its head? (A few people I've met seem to have this feat nailed, too.) Roaches can survive a nuclear blast of radiation up to fifteen times stronger than the amount people can withstand. The little nasties are able to live forty-five minutes underwater and after being frozen for two days. And worst of all, in some instances a female needs to mate only once to lay eggs for the rest of her life. Shudder.

So what do we do if we can't poison, nuke, drown, freeze, or guillotine them? Has anybody tried subjecting them to political speeches? It may not kill 'em but at least it'd drive las cucarachas south of the border during election years.

Like roaches, messiness seems to be a curse some of us struggle to eradicate. Humans must have a clean gene that skips generations. My mother's cleaning fetish hopped right over me but settled squarely on my daughter. Baby Cricket popped out of the womb a clean freak. She would *not* tolerate a dirty diaper and appeared distressed when a drop of juice soiled her spotless bib; whereas my son, Matthew, relished that cozy, warm, squishy feeling in his nappy and loved making mud pies.

As a toddler, Cricket used to sprinkle baby powder all over her room—dresser, toys, closets, inside every drawer—just so she could clean it up.

Matthew, on the other hand, inherited his father's flat feet and my tendency to put off chores today that can better be tackled. . .never. During a temporary lapse in sanity, I spent the night in his college apartment shared by three testosterone-overloaded nineteen-year-old boys. During that Stephen King nightmare, I witnessed bugs the length of my foot lumbering around like Godzilla; discovered a fossilized pterodactyl carcass beneath the bed (okay, maybe it was chicken, but who could tell?); and, while visiting the bathroom, learned what terrible aim baseball stars who never miss on the diamond have (eww!).

My stay at the Adams Family B&B (Bedbugs & Beasties) culminated when I was awakened at 2:00 a.m. by a terrifying sound emanating from the three-day-old pile of dirty dishes in the sink. Whatever was moving in there was big enough to rattle a dinner plate. Gag.

I just can't help but identify with the woman who was incensed by her teenage son's messiness. When he wouldn't wake up one morning, she began tossing random objects at him that were cluttering up his room, including CDs, a football, a coin bank, and an 18-inch samurai knife that—*big* oops!—stuck upright in his buttocks like it was a giant pincushion.

Betcha he got up then!

So what's the answer for us matrons of muddle? How can we grand dames of disarray cope with the ravages of anarchic untidiness and keep our stress thermometers from erupting like Mount Vesuvius?

I've discovered the key: we must lower our expectations. That's right, pitch the perfectionism, lose the legalism, cast off comparisons. Limbo under that self-imposed bar of spotlessness. We're not in competition for the cleanest house award. Who cares if the gal next door's showerhead is shinier than yours?

I'm not saying we should wallow in pigsties, but when we're shackled by perfectionism and controlled by pride, we become slaves to our homes. They own *us* instead of us owning them. Not good. Not wise. Not pleasing to God.

"Don't waste your time on useless work, mere busywork, the barren pursuits of darkness" (Ephesians 5:16 MSG). God wants us to invest our precious minutes on earth in people, not things. Focus on pursuing those whose souls hang in the balance of eternity.

And I don't mean roaches!

Nature abhors a vacuum.
And so do I.

ANNE GIBBONS

Let's Decom-stress

1. Name your Achilles' heel when it comes to messiness. What drives you batty?

2. In the realm of neatness, would you consider yourself a paragon of impeccability, direly deficient, or simply passable? Are you and your family okay with that?

3. Do you ever feel like your home owns you? What steps can you take to transfer ownership back to yourself?

Humility Becomes You
—PRIDE—

Pride lands you flat on your face;
humility prepares you for honors.

PROVERBS 29:23 MSG

It all started when Lisa, the wife of my physical therapist friend Steve, volunteered the two of them to attend a masquerade party as a football player and cheerleader. The catch was, *she* was to be the football player and *he* the cheerleader. This is particularly funny if you know Steve—a very dignified, professional man with a perfectly maintained crew cut and blindingly shiny shoes.

Lisa rounded up pads, helmet, cleats, and a football jersey for her costume, and pom-poms and a megaphone for her husband. But she was completely befuddled about how to locate a cheerleading outfit large enough for all six feet, 160 pounds of Steve.

As Steve amused his patients at the rehab center with his wife's sidelined plans, a large-framed, forty-something woman (built somewhat like a Dallas Cowboys linebacker) volunteered that she happened to have a cheerleading outfit he could borrow. Steve wisely elected *not* to ask why on earth she possessed such a thing, but to appease his wife, he reluctantly took the lady up on her gracious offer.

The weekend before the party, while Lisa was away on a business trip, Steve decided to try on his costume. He tugged and shimmied the one-piece cheerleading dress over his head and down as far as his chest before realizing that he was at an impasse. The fabric was stuck, bunched like a tourniquet, pinning his arms to his sides and rendering him as helpless as a bowling pin.

The oversized blood pressure cuff wouldn't budge. He wiggled and squirmed for twenty minutes, but the stubborn thing wouldn't migrate an inch north or south.

Steve tried to use the phone to call for help, but he couldn't bend his elbows enough to get the receiver to his face. He considered going across the street to get help from the neighbors, but all he was wearing were his boxers and the ridiculous cheerleading outfit that now looked more like a straitjacket. No way to don pants. The police would no doubt arrive before he even made it halfway up the walkway to the doorbell, and his neighbors would certainly never look at him the same again.

He suddenly remembered it was time for his favorite television reality show so, priorities being what they are, Steve punched the remote button with his big toe and hunkered down on the couch. He would much rather watch someone else's reality than deal with his own. There he sat, literally tied up for the following half hour until he realized his hands were going numb.

What to do?

He'd never encountered a problem quite like this in his military career or higher-level education. Certainly not in physical therapy school. He could probably punch 911 with his toes, but explaining the situation to hysterical emergency personnel seemed a little too humbling. In fact, *every* possible solution Steve could think of seemed a little too humbling.

So he prayed. And God brought to mind the story of Samson. "Delilah took new ropes and tied him with them. Then, with men hidden in the room, she called to him, 'Samson, the Philistines are upon you!' But he snapped the ropes off his arms as if they were threads" (Judges 16:12 NIV).

Steve realized he certainly wasn't Schwarzenegger, but he also knew that God is the same yesterday, today, and tomorrow. If the Lord infused Old Testament Samson with supernatural strength to escape an embarrassing situation, maybe He would do the same for twenty-first-century Steve. So he took a deep breath, flexed his muscles, and, to his amazement, ripped through his "new ropes" in Incredible Hulk style.

Of course, he had a lot of explaining to do to the linebacker lady.

Isn't God creative? His versatility with the prideful situations we get ourselves into is truly humbling. He meets us wherever we are—in the church bathroom when we spring a leak, locked out of our car in the rain, or half naked in the gym. Wherever we need Him to bail us out of the stress-pool, He's already there with His bucket.

"But He gives a greater grace. . . . 'God is opposed to the proud, but gives grace to the humble'" (James 4:6 NASB).

Pride is an underhanded thief. It sneaks up and robs us of the heart-changing gratitude that is a byproduct of knowing—and acknowledging—that our attributes, abilities, and accolades are simply gifts from our Creator. Gifts wrapped in love and tied with a bow of grace.

My friend Rich, a teacher and father, has an infectious attitude of humility. When teachers at the Christian school where he worked were told that budget cuts necessitated that staff assume janitorial duties, grumbling broke out among the ranks. During the protests and discussion that ensued, Rich quietly disappeared with the cleaning supplies. When discovered scrubbing toilets on his knees, Rich replied, "Kneeling at this throne is no different than kneeling at God's throne—it's all for His glory!"

> Swallow your pride occasionally;
> it's nonfattening!
>
> UNKNOWN

LET'S DECOM-STRESS

1. Okay, fess up—in which areas of your life do you excel; what are you really good at? Does pride about this accomplishment ever sneak into your attitude or speech? Even a little? If so, with whom?

2. What is God's take on prideful speech in Psalm 59:12? How can we take steps to pluck out the weed of pride before it starts to take over the entire lawn?

3. Has pride ever caused you to refuse instruction or to argue to the death that you're right? What does the Bible have to say about that in Proverbs 13:10?

Smiles to Go Before I Sleep
—SLEEP DEPRIVATION—

When you lie down,
your sleep will be sweet.

PROVERBS 3:24 NIV

Power nap. Oooh, don't those two words send a tingle of anticipation down your spine? The pause that refreshes. Personal mini-vacation. Regrouping. Checking the eyelids for leaks. Stress-unloading. Closing up shop. Catching our breath.

Whatever you call it, women need it. Want it. Will bust a few heads to get it.

My newest political agenda is to petition Congress to legislate a daily American siesta, something like the custom followed in many European countries. We could close down all businesses from 1:00 to 3:00 p.m., curl up on little mats like kindergartners (after mandatory cookies and milk, of course), catch some zzz's, and become a kinder, gentler nation because of it.

Think of all the road rage we'd avoid!

In my humble but accurate opinion, happy naps are an essential cause-pause in the nonstop stress of our day. They're little slices of heaven that revive our energy, clarity, and motivation; our front line of defense against temperament-ravaging fatigue, which results in acute nastiness.

When I miss my nappy, ain't nobody happy.

And I'm not alone. Ladies, without our happy naps, we're all reduced to two-year-olds. I believe that consciousness is simply that annoying time between naps.

Remember your kindergartner complaining about having to take a nap because *you* wanted to? My response? Children and old ladies (I was twenty-nine at the time) *must* take naps. It's the law. We don't want the nap police coming to our door, now, do we?

What about *guilt*, you ask. No *way*, I say. Remember, the almighty Creator of the universe set the precedent by resting after a strenuous workweek. I picture Him curling up on a fluffy white cloud, cuddling the koala bear He'd just created, smiling down at the sparkling new earth and all the freshly named critters. And wishing He'd skipped head lice.

Anyhow, Papa God never meant for us to keep going nine hundred miles per hour all day. He built triggers into our bodies to cue us when it's time to escape consciousness. Wise people listen to these cues, such as notable nappers Albert Einstein, Thomas Edison, Winston Churchill, John F. Kennedy, and Ronald Reagan.

There's good reason why our eyelids start to droop around 2:00 p.m. (Hey, I haven't been in the medical field thirty years for nothing!) The levator muscles that constantly contract to keep our eyelids open while we're awake finally poop out and beg for a break.

Also, a chemical called *adenosine* collects in our brains while we're awake, which piles up and makes us feel drowsy. Our bodies yearn for sleep to allow the adenosine to disseminate. The resulting euphoric feeling is similar to the instant relief that comes from emptying your full bladder (thought you'd identify with that!).

A study published in the Annals of Internal Medicine showed that people who nap at least thirty minutes a day, three times a week, are one-third less likely to die from heart disease. Plus, research suggests that taking a nap can boost creativity and memory. Cognitive neuroscientist William Fishbein reports that during *slow-wave sleep*—the period of deep sleep that comes just before REM (dream time)—a state often achieved with a power nap, our brains actually keep working to solve problems and come up with new ideas.

Mozart claimed to have composed music in his dreams. Keith Richards found "Satisfaction" while snoozing, too. Our brains run on autopilot while we free-fall. It's like a doughnut machine that keeps plopping out crullers even when unplugged.

And there's an even bigger argument for my case! Research shows that a little extra sleep can help with weight control—yup, you can lose as you snooze! (No, I *didn't* dream this up!) *Ghrelin*, a hormone produced in our intestines, clues us in that we're hungry and sparks cravings for sweets, starches, and salty foods.

When we don't get enough sleep, ghrelin levels rise. So we eat. Lots of naughty stuff, which can lead to obesity, depression, raccoon eyes (dark circles), headaches, impatience, and irritability.

You know, our usual quirks.

But when we sleep more, our colons stockpile less ghrelin, our naughty cravings diminish, and we stuff those guts with fewer Twinkies. From my perspective, it's a simple formula: $S = N + H - C$ (Skinny equals Naps plus Hormones minus Calories).

All this scientific talk led me to formulate another Coty near-fact of science, the BOOP Theory (okay, maybe I *did* make this one up).

I postulate that women are like pots of oatmeal. At the beginning of the day we simmer—little manageable bubbles of stress rise to the surface and dissipate as they harmlessly pop. But as the day progresses, the heat escalates and the oatmeal boils higher and wilder and meaner until it overflows and spoils its surroundings with a sticky, ugly, nasty mess. That would be me about 4:00 p.m.

Napping prevents BOOP (Boiling Oatmeal Overflow Phenomenon) by turning off the burner to allow the oatmeal to calm down to a pleasant, servable consistency. Sprinkle on a dab of brown sugar and voilá—everybody's happy.

The Bible records numerous times that Jesus Himself stole away for a rest break and encouraged His buds to do likewise. So I'm encouraging *you* with a little pseudo-poetry:

Ode to Napping
By D. Coty, poet extraordinaire

If your afternoon bloop
is gobbledy-gook
from experiencing BOOP
because you're just pooped,
for the good of the troop,
step out of the loop
until you regroup
and the fam can recoup!

Set aside half an hour every day to do all your worrying,
then take a nap during this period.

UNKNOWN

LET'S DECOM-STRESS

1. Are you a happy napper? If so, how do you slip away? If not, why not consider a quiet time instead? Read Mark 6:30–32. Why do you think stealing away for rest was so important to Jesus? Why is it important for you?

2. I often awaken with great story ideas in my head. Have you ever experienced problem solving or creative processing in your sleep? Isn't it just too cool how Papa God wired us to park the car while the engine's still running?

3. Has BOOP ever ruined your afternoon? Brainstorm ways to turn down the heat on your pot of oatmeal before it overflows.

Things My Mother Never Told Me
—MENOPAUSE—

I know everything you have done,
and you are not cold or hot.
I wish you were either one or the other.

REVELATION 3:15 CEV

Did someone turn up the furnace?

I was sitting among fifteen men and women at Bible study, our chairs drawn into a tight circle. On my right was Spouse; on my left was a single man I barely knew. Suddenly, out of the clear blue, a volcano of invisible molten lava erupted from my innards, spreading its scorching flow from my toenails to my hair follicles.

Oh no! Hot flash alert!

Sitting there smoldering like a red-hot charcoal, I tried to ignore that I was a hunka hunka burning love, acting nonchalant about the inferno beneath my skin and the perspiration beading on my forehead. I felt as if I were glowing like a 1,000-watt bulb. Heat fumes radiated from my pores, and dampness formed half-circles around my armpits. My belt was literally a ring of fire. Makeup dripped down my face and glued my chins together. When my reading glasses slid off the end of my nose onto my open Bible with a thud, the clueless dude beside me sniffed the air quizzically and asked, "Is something burning?"

Heads shook all around, but Spouse's knowing eyes cut toward me. As the Bible study leader resumed the lesson, Chuck casually began flipping pages in his Bible, discreetly fanning me with the resulting breeze.

What a guy! I never loved him more than at that moment.

You know, you'd think we could at least lose weight from all that sweating. Why aren't there legions of skinny, water-soluble, fifty-something-year-old women walking around? We should all look like emaciated size 2 supermodels. It's the least God could do to make it up to us.

Men intentionally don't understand "the change." It sounds too permanent. Most husbands think menopause is like a PAUSE button with a DVD (more like *mental pause*), just a phase they must endure. A brief, temporary insanity their wives go through while the comfortable marriage they once knew is inconveniently on hold.

They thought they'd seen it all during the crazy, absentminded days of pregnancy: shoes in the silverware drawer, milk in the dishwasher, a plate of watermelon and black olives for dinner. She *must* have pickles today although she detested them last week. Sweaters in June, flip-flops in February.

Then thirty years later they walk into the kitchen to find Hot Flash Fannie with a baggie of frozen chicken legs tucked into the waistband of her jeans so they'll defrost in time for dinner. (I actually did this after reading Martha Bolton's *Cooking with Hot Flashes!*) Or she's crying hysterically at the bird feeder because the baby wrens left their mama for the first time. Or she's chowing down on a vat of mocha-almond ice cream swimming in a pool of hot fudge and chocolate sprinkles. For breakfast. Or she's spread-eagled, buck naked on the cold bathroom tile floor at 3:00 a.m. with steam rising all around her.

Yup. The milk's back in the dishwasher (only this time it's skim), her purse is chilling nicely in the refrigerator, and she's mean as a snake because. . .well, just *because*! There's no rhyme or reason—or warning—when her grumplitude will suddenly soar off the charts.

Grumplitude? Girl, you know grumplitude; you just didn't know what to call it. In my book *Mom NEEDS Chocolate*, I introduced this scale of attitudinal grumpiness that fluctuates in direct relation to a woman's (a) blood sugar, (b) hormones, and (c) sleep tank. If the grumplitude gauge is on E, the fam hauls out the big-game tranquilizer dart rifle and takes cover behind the furniture.

The worst part for women is that we know we're being irrational and irritable, but we can't seem to stop ourselves. It's like we're channeling Godzilla and there's no remote to change channels. (Hey, if she were a male she'd have been called

Godzillo.) Menopausal tempers tend to metamorph (this is not really a word but it should be) and we get a little, well, shall we say, *crisp* in our response delivery. Like a snapping crocodile.

To prevent this and other alarming what-in-the-world-will-I-do-next surprises, I offer up this menopausal morning prayer:

Lord, please chill my internal inferno and help me not to have an ity day. You know, an uppity day in which I demonstrate, in no particular order, density, banality, crudity, calamity, stupidity, disunity, ferocity, futility, audacity, and especially insanity. And thank You for Your gracious generosity. Amen.

There's hidden wisdom in the old joke:

Q: What should a man do while his wife is going through menopause?

A: Keep busy. Finish the basement. When you're done you'll have a place to live.

Is it any wonder we're chronically grumpy when we have to keep doing things, like applying makeup, during a hot flash?

For some reason, middle-aged female bodies excel in engulfing themselves in flames when they arise from bed in the mornings. Even after washing and patting our faces dry, perspiration continues to ooze from every facial pore so that foundation clots into little beige warts along the cheekbones. We try to flatten out the warts as we apply powder, but the powder puff gets cakey and it ends up leaving a smear streaking up the nose and across the forehead like a Seminole warrior preparing for battle.

Then instead of lightly highlighting our cheekbones, blush sticks to the first clammy spot it touches, creating a round rosy splotch that makes us look more feverish than festive. Mercy. I've always wanted to be considered a living doll, but please, not Raggedy Ann!

Another little known true scientific ditty about menopause (you're gonna *love* this!): as our estrogen supply wanes, our bodies are wired to replace it with *phenylethylamine*, the hormone produced by cocao. That's right, chocolate. Can you believe it? Papa God thought of everything. Hey, if your car's gas tank is empty, you fill it to keep the car running, right? Same thing with hormones. If regular-grade estrogen isn't available, high-test cocoa will do nicely. And Swiss truffle premium produces optimum engine performance!

Who says change has to be bad, anyway? I kind of like the idea of reinventing

a wiser (even rats learn), sexier (think full-bodied fine wines here), more robust (aged cheddar is everybody's favorite) version of myself. According to Genesis 12, Abraham's wife, Sarah, was a real hottie at sixty-five. Foreign kings lusted after her, and Abe lied that she was his sister to keep his head on his shoulders when competition escalated.

So, girls, let's think of ourselves as hotties, too. And we *are*. We literally sizzle.

Now it's time to sing along with Mitch (my nickname in college—my maiden name was Mitchell). A brand-new theme song just for my hottie gal pals!

Menopause the Attitude-y-full

(Sing to the tune of "America the Beautiful")

O beau-ti-ful, those choc-olate pies,
Frap-pes, lat-tes, and more.
For Met-a-mu-cil, fail-ing eyes,
And cell-u-lite galore;
O men-o-pause,
O men-o-pause,
Take thy hor-mones and flee.
I'll douse thy mood
With scads of food
And mounds of mocha cream.

(So sorry—for the sake of space I'm limited here to the first verse and chorus, but I'd be delighted to share the rest of this and my other gal goony-tunes with you and your gang at your next upcoming event. Please see page 255 for scheduling information.)

Age is something that doesn't matter,
unless you are a cheese.
BILLIE BURKE, AKA GLINDA THE
GOOD WITCH IN *THE WIZARD OF OZ*

LET'S DECOM-STRESS

1. I don't mean to scare you if you're not yet facing the changing mode of life. Not every woman has hot flashes. Did your mom? Your grandmom? Your '87 Chevy? (Hold on to this book—you're gonna need this chapter one day!)

2. For those of you who are already certified hotties, did you ever wonder why you crave chocolate? You've got a great reason—your body needs phenylethylamine to keep that engine purring! Explain *that* to the little mister and see if he doesn't magically produce a box of Godiva after dinner tonight.

3. Okay, if you haven't already, belt out a few choruses of "Menopause the Attitude-y-full." Don't you feel a lot less *ity* already?

You Can Run but You Can't Hide
—God's Mercy—

When my life was slipping away,
I remembered you—
and in your holy temple you
heard my prayer.

JONAH 2:7 CEV

"What's *wrong* with this fool dog?" my husband, Chuck, wondered aloud as the fluffy white Maltese eluded his grasp yet again.

We had been doggie-sitting my sister Cindy's canine pack for a week, and as a special treat (for the dog, not us!), I'd brought Savannah, Cindy's beloved five-pound bundle of wispy hair, to our house seven doors down. I thought the little dear would enjoy destroying our living room while I got ready for a book signing. Rushing away late as usual, I hollered to Chuck, who was working in his home office, to please return Savannah to Cindy's house at his first opportunity.

"Uh-huh," he muttered, focused on his computer screen.

Ten minutes later, a UPS man rang the doorbell. Forgetting about our furry visitor, Chuck opened the door and Savannah zipped right through his legs into the front yard. Stashing the package just inside the doorway, Chuck rushed after his naughty little charge and she, alarmed by his groping hands, took off down the sidewalk at an expeditious clip.

She must be headed home, Chuck thought, leaving the door standing open and our own two dogs roaming the yard. *I'll just head her off and be back in a flash.*

Well, whatever destiny was in Savannah's pea-sized brain, it wasn't home. She bolted around Chuck and scurried right past her own house toward an intersection. Chuck followed at a dead run, first cajoling in his *nice* voice then in his stern Daddy voice. When nothing else worked, he just plain yelled, but the determined little dog kept five paces ahead of him, cagily avoiding his lunging fingertips.

Chuck blanched as Savannah darted through the intersection. Car brakes squealed and taillights flared, but the tiny canine pressed on as if on a mission. A half mile later, with winded Chuck trying desperately to keep up, Savannah cut through a yard into a thirty-acre strawberry field bordered on the far end by dense woods and an alligator-infested lake.

By this time, Chuck was panting and sweaty and a few fries short of a Happy Meal. He helplessly watched the furball that Cindy considered her precious baby disappear beneath long rows of leafy strawberry plants, much taller than Savannah.

Panicked, Chuck ignored the stitch in his side and raced home for the car. Our neighbor kindly consented to round up our dogs, who had happily accepted this golden opportunity to tour the neighborhood, while Chuck headed for the strawberry farm. Approaching the farmer and his workers tending the fields, Chuck explained his dilemma and asked permission to drive through the property toward the lake.

"Go ahead, but there's no need to hurry," the crusty old farmer replied, spitting into the dirt. "Gators probably already had 'er for lunch."

With dread cementing his guts, Chuck combed the acreage in the blazing Florida sun, screaming Savannah's name more urgently as the minutes ticked by. Five, ten, then fifteen. He shot machine-gun prayers heavenward while his mind reeled.

"Do You really care about stubborn, rebellious creatures like Savannah, Father?

"Why should the Lord of heaven and earth waste His time rescuing hapless victims of their own bad choices?

"Savannah certainly doesn't deserve Your mercy. But if You don't intervene, Lord, what'll I tell Cindy about the pet she loved more than anything? How about,

'I'm so sorry, but while you entrusted your darling little Fru-Fru to our care, she became a reptilian's hors d'oeuvre?'"

Just then, a flash of white caught Chuck's eye at the edge of the woods. Could it be?

Praise the Lord, it was! Savannah, long snowy hair flying in the breeze, bounded through wild palmetto shrubs like her tail was afire. Chuck drove as close as he could without scaring her away. The last thing he wanted to do was drive her deeper into the woods or closer to the lake.

Although he yearned to wring her wee little neck, Chuck cautiously opened the car door, ducked out of sight, and called out in his merriest, falsetto, Cindy-imitation southern drawl (which was quite a stretch for a bass-singing New Yorker), "Yoo-hoo! Sweetie-pie-Savannah-baby-girl, how about a yummy bone-si-poo? Come to Mama!"

Whether Savannah was truly fooled or if she decided Uncle Chuck was slightly less frightening than a three hundred-pound lizard or if she had just grown tired of her little adventure, we'll never know. After hesitating only briefly, she trotted over and jumped into the car.

When Chuck later regaled us with this wayward doggie tale (or is that "tail"?), I couldn't help but think of Old Testament Jonah. While fleeing willy-nilly from God, Jonah's poor decisions resulted in his being ingested by a monstrous water-dwelling creature. He was flying by the seat of his pants with no real destination, no plan B, no escape contingency. He was just blindly reacting to something he didn't want to do, hightailing it anywhere but *there*. Without God's intervention, he would have merely ended up a seafood appetizer.

Jehovah chose to overlook Jonah's hardheaded disobedience and rescue his bony behind anyway. That, girlfriend, is mercy.

And what about me? What about you? We're no different than Savannah or Jonah. We, too, run away from difficult places or daunting tasks or annoying people God has placed in our lives. The same questions apply: Why does God care about stubborn, rebellious creatures? Why should He waste His time rescuing hapless victims of their own bad choices? We certainly don't deserve His mercy.

Yet He lovingly extends it to us anyway. Over and over and over again.

Those who loved you and were helped by you will remember you when forget-me-nots have withered. Carve your name on hearts, not marble.

CHARLES SPURGEON

LET'S DECOM-STRESS

1. Receiving Papa God's mercy is like opening a note from someone you've offended and finding a five-hundred-dollar gift card to your favorite shoe store. When was the last time you experienced His incomprehensible mercy and forgiveness?

2. Mercy is completely undeserved; I think that's what makes it so exquisitely valuable. Take a moment to treasure the free gift of God's mercy in giving His Son as payment for your sins. Wrap mercy around your shoulders like a thick fleece blanket and soak up its warmth.

3. Is there someone who has wronged you and deserves punishment? How can you show him or her mercy like your Father has shown you?

Cheesecake: Not Just for Breakfast Anymore
—NUTRITION—

The righteous eat to their hearts' content, but the stomach of the wicked goes hungry.

PROVERBS 13:25 NIV

I stared at the decadent pastries in the coffee shop display case.

"The chewy gooey fudge cake looks good today," the lady in line behind me observed.

"Definitely," I agreed, wiping a drop of drool from the corner of my mouth. "But I really shouldn't. I'm dieting and haven't been a very good girl this week." I tried to look contrite and, above all, sincere. "I think I'll go with a low-fat bran muffin."

She raised one eyebrow. Apparently, I wasn't fooling anyone.

"Or maybe I'll splurge with the sugar-free, faux apple cake," I conceded with a shrug, "although I'd sure rather have a jumbo slice of that chocolate-raspberry cheesecake."

My newly found kindred spirit leaned close and looked me conspiratorially in the eyes. "Diet, schmiet. Listen, if you're going to cheat on your husband, don't pick an ugly man."

Weight control is no piece of cake. You know it's true: sugar shows and money talks, but chocolate sings! I've found that a big ole hunk of peanut butter fudge is the best way to gag that obnoxious skinny inner gal trying to bust through the waist rolls.

Even science acknowledges our propensity for muffin-stuffin'.

Who's surprised that a study by the Brookhaven National Laboratory found that when presented their favorite foods, women are less able than men to subdue their hunger, even using "cognitive inhibition" techniques to help squelch cravings? It seems that women's brain scans showed insuppressible neuron activity at the sight of exciting goodies, regardless of all attempts to block it.

I thought Pavlov proved that with his slobbery dogs a long time ago. They must have been girl dogs. Why, drool gushes from my lips at the very mention of chocolate chunk cookies; you certainly don't have to show me a picture, much less ring a bell. You need to douse a fire? I'm your girl. Just suspend me over the blaze and read me a Death by Chocolate recipe.

Isn't it simply polite to answer when certain foods call our name?

I recently read that our personalities are reflected in our snacks of choice. For instance, potato chips are chosen by ambitious, competitive people, whereas tortilla chips are selected by perfectionists who tend to take charge and micromanage. Conscientious people with high principles tend to scarf cheese curls, and pretzels are the fave crave of the fashionable and trendy.

Hey, maybe instead of the traditional four personality types (choleric, sanguine, melancholic, and phlegmatic), we should switch to tortilla, pretzel, cheese curl, or potato chip. Women would certainly understand the implications better.

"Hi. I'm Debbie, a cheese curl girl. This is my husband, Chuck." Lean close and whisper knowingly, "He's a *tortilla* guy."

I've always felt that it's a logical stress reliever and only fair to attribute proper nutritional value to vegetable-based snack foods. Why impose more munchy confusion on our crazy mixed-up world than already exists? After all, what's in corn chips if not corn? Tortillas are basically flat, crispy corn bread, right? And what could be wrong with *potato* chips? They're not apple pie chips or ice cream chips (which, if they existed, should be considered in the fruit and dairy categories rather than junk food).

We mustn't let our sense of humor be the first thing we lose on our diets.

In our society, dieting is as much a part of womanhood as plucking chin hairs. It is said that diets are the penalty for exceeding the feed limit. Can you believe that the American Heart Association advises women to consume no more than 100 calories of sugar per day? That's the equivalent of six teaspoons. Mercy, that's only half a Snickers!

An average American swallows twenty-two teaspoons of sugar daily, largely from soft drinks or, in the genteel South, sweet tea. So if I skip the tea and drink water for dinner, can I have an extra brownie? I'd rather chew my calories than guzzle them, anyway. I'm thinking if I plant sugarcane in my backyard, I might be able to get away with gnawing on a sliver after meals, like men chew on toothpicks. The calories probably wouldn't even count. What could be more "natural" than a sweet-toothpick, I ask you?

But you know as well as I do that after going through all the blood, sweat, and baby carrots that go into losing weight, gaining it back is the devil's last laugh. You can almost feel his rancid breath on your neck as he chuckles wickedly over your shoulder at the spinning dial on the scale. Erma Bombeck once quipped, "In two decades I've lost a total of 789 pounds. I should be hanging from a charm bracelet."

I applaud those sisters who consume nutritionally sound diets and avoid creating waist baskets. For you ultra-disciplined gals, I say, "You go, girl!" But for the rest of us, I've got one word: *chill*. That's right, relax. Take a deep breath. Un-wedgie your underwear. Let your bra out a notch. Unbutton your pants. Remember, these earth suits are only temporary. Heaven will not have beauty pageants. And I really don't think it would be heaven without Oreos.

It's a crying shame to devote our lives to the goal of standing at the door to eternity with gorgeous size 4 bodies, tanned to perfection, foreheads silky-smooth, eyes bag-free, hair gleaming, arms Dumbo flapless, thighs tapioca-free. What good is that? God will not be impressed. He'll be looking at our insides, at our hearts.

No, in my opinion we should be wheel-barrowed to the grave with a goofy grin on our faces, clutching Cadbury in one hand and Cheetos in the other.

No diet will remove all the fat from your body because the brain is entirely fat. Without a brain, you might look good, but all you could do is run for public office.

GEORGE BERNARD SHAW

LET'S DECOM-STRESS

1. So which personality type are you: tortilla, pretzel, cheese curl, or potato chip? Or maybe a combo platter?

2. Are you a successful weight-loser, yo-yo dieter, or nutritionally sound eater? Do you feel that your current method of food consumption adds stress to your life?

3. Has your focus been on decorating your earth suit? What steps can you take to shift emphasis to the inside rather than the outside?

Girls Just Need to Have Fun
—STRESS RELIEF—

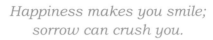

Happiness makes you smile;
sorrow can crush you.

PROVERBS 15:13 CEV

Do you know the one stress reliever that women need every day but often neglect? Nope, it's not love, sex, or chocolate engorgement, although those things definitely rank in the top ten.

Are you ready? It's *fun*! That's right—good ole giggle-producing, endorphin-generating, tension-popping fun!

Need proof? Stop a minute and take this little zest test:

1. What is your favorite outlet for expressing creativity?
2. Name your happiest memory of participating in the above activity.
3. If you could do anything today just for fun, what would it be?
4. When was the last time you laughed till your cheeks ached?
5. What was your favorite thing to do as a kid? Have you done it lately?
6. Which current peer activities provide you with a satisfying sense of togetherness?
7. Who are the two friends you most enjoy hanging with?
8. What or who makes you laugh more than anything else in the world?
9. How does listening to your favorite music make you feel?
10. What exciting place do you look forward to going to one day?

You're smiling now, aren't you? Feel your heart floating in your chest? The load on your shoulders lighten up? Don't you feel like you've swallowed an antiaging vitamin just thinking about these happiness-inducing sources that leave frenzy behind?

Studies show that there are definite correlations between enjoyable activities and stress reduction. In fact, stress management professionals recommend that you engage in at least one activity weekly just for fun. But, hey, why stop at one?

Not only are fun activities a key stress-coping mechanism, but cultivating relaxing hobbies provides a way to express yourself, sharpen latent talents (or develop skills you always wished you had), and release pent-up angst. We may not be able to eliminate stress from our crazy lives, but we *can* empower ourselves to weather the stress better by pursuing rejuvenating activities that refill our joy tanks rather than suck us bone dry.

We all desire to be productive, but I've found that all work and no play makes Deb pig out. How about you? Do you reach for comfort food when your nerves are frayed and good judgment is weakened? Well, that's the wrong kind of productivity—all we produce is jiggly thighs. There must be something non-fattening that's productive *and* fun to do, right?

After years of accommodating everyone else in our families, many of us grow out of touch with what *we* like to do. Here are some suggestions that many gals adore:

- Do some gardening. It reconnects you with God's amazing creation; lets you explore fresh avenues of color, texture, and sensory creativity in a calming environment; and allows you to nurture new life (sooo fulfilling!). Plants enable you to beautify your personal space and provide lots of regenerating oxygen to your little world.
- Participate in sports. A socially acceptable way to release frustration. (Better than beating up your trash can or shredding your panty hose.) Also a great way to deepen relationships, exercise, and work off a few white chocolate macadamia nut cookies. If you're not the competitive type, you don't even have to *play* anything; you can walk, run, dance, do aerobics, skate, or bike with girlfriends or even your spouse (a double-header investment in your marriage and your health). According to marriage expert Willard F. Harley Jr. in *His Needs, Her Needs*, "Among the five basic male needs, spending recreational time with his wife is second only to sex for the typical husband."

Hmm. Who knows? Maybe one recreational activity will lead to the other!

- Find your creative outlet. Draw, sing, knit, craft, scrapbook, work puzzles, paint, write, cook, scuba dive, explore photography—the list is as diverse as your interests. Taking classes and trying different things not only expands your skill set, but increases your self-esteem and stocks you up with interesting conversation ammo for those awkward "now what?" silences at get-togethers.

- Laugh! See funny movies, read hilarious books, associate with light-minded people, and search for humor in life's everyday situations. This proactive lighten-up formula not only produces a positive frame of mind; it transforms your unintentional scowl into a smiley face and naturally attracts others to you. Laughter reflects a joyful heart! Who doesn't like to hang with joyful, uplifting people?

- Enjoy music. Take piano lessons (I love teaching adults—they learn quickly and truly value musical self-expression), pull out your old high school band instrument and join a community orchestra, or listen to music you love. Boogie. Belly dance. Polka. Get your bad self down. Music has the magical ability to speed us up, calm us down, distract (in a good way), and inspire us— tap into this simple source of happiness (pun intended)!

- Fall into the pages of a good book. Nonfiction. Fiction. Biographies of amazing people. Christian fantasy. Inspirational romance. Mysteries. Faith-centered novels are an invigorating escape into another life, even another world. Just don't forget to come back. . . .

- Seek adventure. Plan and save for those special vacations. Anticipation is half the fun. Having something exciting to look forward to expands the imagination and quickens the heart like nothing else. I've been waiting for my European adventure for a decade now, and the anticipation only grows sweeter each passing year.

- Take mini-vacations. Long weekends or even day trips are great fun if time and money are an issue. Visit that quaint bed-and-breakfast nearby or the museum you've never seen, spend a day at the beach, go window shopping with a friend, or relax around a campfire beneath a starlit sky with those you love. Just don't forget the bug spray.

- Get involved in a cause you believe in. This can be fulfilling and fun if you make sure it doesn't become work. The goal here is refreshment—not more drudgery.

About now you're probably thinking, *I shouldn't be wasting time doing those things for myself. I have my family to take care of.* C'mon, now, shed the guilt, sister—fun is good for you *and* your family members! You're investing in your health and future, which directly affects their health and futures as well.

Scientists have proven that laughter increases circulation and exercises skeletal muscles (unfortunately that includes sphincter muscles if you laugh too hard!). One study I read about confirmed that laughing fifteen minutes every morning for three weeks significantly increased optimism, positive emotions, social identification, and. . .um, regulation.

Bye-bye, prune juice.

Fun is actually contagious! A British medical journal concluded from social experiments that happiness transferred between people can last up to a year. A year! When you smile, the whole world really *does* smile with you!

My friend Jan was jockeying a cart containing her toddler grandson, Mason, through Walmart when they overtook a stooped old man inching his buggy along, his elderly wife shuffling behind him with weary eyes and sagging shoulders. As they passed the somber couple, Mason placed a chubby little hand over his mouth and blew them the biggest, loudest kiss you'd ever want to catch. Two worn, wrinkled faces instantly transformed as they returned giggles and air kisses the rest of the way down the aisle.

Remember, Solomon, the wisest guy who ever lived, agreed: "I've decided that there's nothing better to do than go ahead and have a good time and get the most we can out of life" (Ecclesiastes 3:12 MSG). So make it a point to add a little frolic to your to-do list and start looking forward to tomorrow!

The more I've watched the connection between humor and creativity, the more I've realized there is very little difference between the terms "Aha!" and "Ha–ha!"

VATCHE BARTEKIAN, STRESS MANAGEMENT SPECIALIST

LET'S DECOM-STRESS

1. What does Proverbs 17:22 tell us about the importance of having fun?

2. Which new fun activity sounds like something you'd like to explore?

3. Do you ever struggle with guilt about spending time doing things you enjoy? What is keeping you from scheduling these activities on a regular basis?

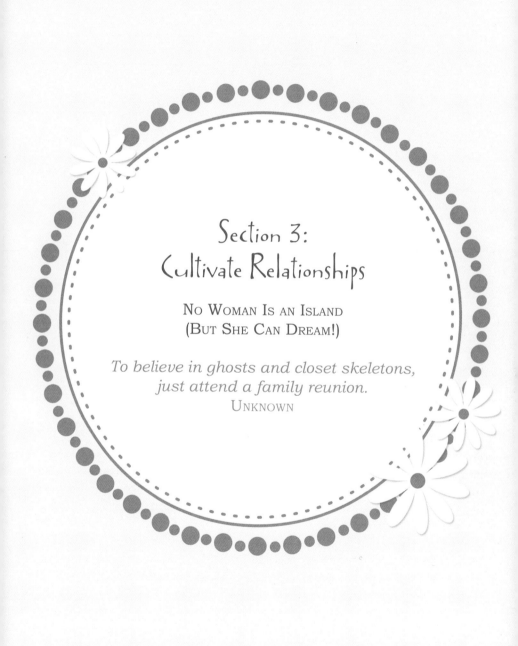

Section 3:
Cultivate Relationships

NO WOMAN IS AN ISLAND
(BUT SHE CAN DREAM!)

*To believe in ghosts and closet skeletons,
just attend a family reunion.*
UNKNOWN

Romancing the Drone
—ROMANCE—

For this reason a man shall leave
his father and his mother, and be joined to
his wife; and they shall become one flesh.

GENESIS 2:24 NASB

The newspapers said it all: "A man fighting with his girlfriend clung to a car roof and punched her through the window as she drove more than a mile on a busy road" (*Tampa Tribune*, February 25, 2009).

"When his wife needed a kidney transplant, Richard Batista gave her one of his. Now that Dawnell Batista has filed for divorce, Richard wants his kidney back as part of his settlement" (*Tampa Tribune*, January 8, 2009).

"A man who woke up and found his head bleeding drove to work and left a note for his boss before going to the hospital to find he had a bullet lodged in his brain. . . . His girlfriend later apparently killed herself when contacted by police" (*Tampa Tribune*, December 28, 2005).

Headlines like these give romance a black eye. Literally. Stress-filled, dysfunctional relationships are just what women *don't* need. We read romance novels, devour tabloid love stories, watch romantic movies, and deliriously dish about happily-ever-after scenarios, but it can get depressing when real-life romance seems to be just a fairy tale.

Perhaps romance doesn't *have* to be illusive—if we just tweak it a little.

On the Orango Island off the western coast of Africa, it's customary for women to propose. What a great idea! The gals choose their fellas, then propose by offering their grooms-to-be a special dish of fish marinated in red palm oil. They don't have to worry about rejection because the men *always* accept (how's that for de-stressing a relationship?). To refuse would dishonor their families, and besides, it's an accepted fact that, as one islander married for fifty years puts it, "Love comes first into the heart of the woman. Once it's in the woman, only then can it jump into the man."

Preach it, brother.

Alas, Western cultural mores are seeping into the ways of the island, and men are beginning to pursue women. As we know all too well, the lust leech sometimes overpowers the love bug.

"The choice of a woman is much more stable," islander Cesar Okrane, age ninety, concedes. "Rarely were there divorces before. Now, with men choosing, divorce has become common."

Could these people know something our techno-advanced, sophisticated, 60 percent divorce-rated society doesn't? Could men and women view romance differently?

I mean, one glimpse at nature confirms what we already know about the male gender. Didn't you ever wonder why God made the male cardinal's crimson plumage so dramatically brilliant while the females are garbed with duller-than-dishwater motifs? It's like the boy birds are decked out with tuxedos while the girls get stuck with housecoats. The males flit around showing off their flashy duds while the females are busy vacuuming the nest and frying worm burgers for the wee chicklets.

And cardinals aren't the only birds fixated on appearances.

In a scientific study published in *Current Biology* (June 2008 issue), a Magic Marker was used to darken the rust-colored breast feathers of male New Jersey barn swallows in order to test the female reaction. Apparently clothes make the man in the aviary world as well, for the males' testosterone level increased significantly within one week of getting their makeovers. Those dudes must have been feeling pretty plucky about themselves, and the gals apparently considered them studlier, too, for mating statistics flew sky high.

But, as every woman who has married a slim man whose hair was actually on his head and not bristling from every other surface on his potbellied body twenty years later knows, looks aren't everything. Being *hot* has nothing to do with marriage. Hey, tamales and hell are *hot*!

Other qualities are more important. Loyalty. Devotion. Picking up stinky socks. Why, look at the knot-tying weaverbird (you can tell this gal's organized by her very name!). She proves that slobbery is *not* acceptable by refusing to mate with a messy-nested male. Our girl won't even lift a feather until her prospective beau rips down his squalid, subpar condor-minium and rebuilds it to her neatness specifications.

We can learn something from critters, don't you think? Job was on to something when he said, "Ask the animals, and they will teach you" (Job 12:7 NIV).

And how 'bout those California fiddler crabs? The crabby gals (no, that doesn't include you or me) check out an average of twenty-three boy crabs and their burrows before choosing a mate. Crab cribs are obviously pretty important to discretionary lady crustaceans. They don't bunk down with just anybody. Shouldn't that be the case with two-legged, non-crusty humanoids?

After all, what's wrong with being choosy in our relationships? Isn't that the underlying message of 2 Corinthians 6:15? "How can a believer be a partner with an unbeliever?" (NLT). Shared faith is often the glue that holds a dry and shriveling relationship together until it can be reconditioned. Our Lord specializes in repairing rips in relationships. He's more than happy to provide the marital cord strength when two of the strands become frayed: "A cord of three strands is not quickly torn apart" (Ecclesiastes 4:12 NASB).

Yes, romance is based on a lot more than wine and roses. Or soda and wieners, for that matter. I once heard a man introduce his spouse as "my trophy wife." When asked why he used that term, he looked adoringly at his wife and replied with a big smile, "Because I won the prize!" What a wonderful way for a man to view love!

According to 1 Corinthians 13:4–6, true romantic love is rooted in the unconditional acceptance God demonstrates toward us:

> Love is kind and patient, never
> jealous, boastful, proud, or rude.
> Love isn't selfish or quick tempered.
> It doesn't keep a record of wrongs that others do.
> Love rejoices in the truth, but not in evil. (CEV)

Wow! What a list of romance-enhancers! Imagine the potential of a relationship where both partners are kind and patient with one another, never rude or pouty or resentful. A true partnership where hurt feelings don't compound and previous mistakes are totally forgiven and forgotten. Where truth is the norm and transparency is not risky.

This heavenly model—which describes the way the Lover of our souls treats us—is our goal for optimal earthly relationships. A stress-free, safe haven to give and give and give all the love that overflows from our hearts. *Eros* love, the passionate, romantic type of love that God created specially for a unique bond between a man and woman.

Ah, romance is in the air!

So the next time your fella gets out that Magic Marker to spruce up his feathers a bit, swash a dab of red palm oil in the fish fryer and get ready to rumble!

You don't love someone for their looks
or their clothes or for their fancy car,
but because they sing a song only you can hear.

UNKNOWN

LET'S DECOM-STRESS

1. Reflect for a moment on the best romantic experience of your life (I'm talking emotional here—connecting hearts—not necessarily physical.) You're grinning now, girl, aren't you? Love can do that for us!

2. What were the elements that made that romantic moment so special?

3. How can you incorporate Ecclesiastes 4:12 into your current relationship to make it the strongest and longest union of all?

....

....

....

....

....

....

....

....

....

....

....

....

....

Nuts in the Batter
—DEALING WITH DIFFICULT PEOPLE—

Don't hit back;
discover beauty in everyone.
ROMANS 12:17 MSG

A millionaire in my city recently made "World's Worst Neighbor" headlines. After an ongoing dispute with his neighbor in the adjacent mansion of a ritzy, exclusive golfing community, this highly respected businessman began phoning threatening messages to his nemesis at 5:00 one Sunday morning. He then drove his golf cart into the neighbor's four-car garage (apparently after breaking in) and pounded on his door.

That didn't create enough of a bang, so he launched M-80 fireworks into the guy's yard. No kidding.

You've dealt with a few yourself, haven't you? Difficult people—boils on the hindquarters of humanity, dreary bores, irritating complainers, thorns in your side, vexing nuisances, nasty adversaries, annoying troublemakers. . .all summed up as NIBs (Nuts in the Batter).

NIBs exist in every walk of life: rich, poor, old, young; all shapes, sizes, and sexes. Some are relatives, some strangers. (Some stranger than others.) Many deserve the title (face it, we all earn a NIB sash and tiara at some time or another). A few have it bestowed upon them prematurely. But all NIBs have one thing in common: selfish behavior that grates our last raw nerve.

Thinking about NIBs brings to mind a primate study I read about recently. Don't you just love the transparency of animals—they're like naked humans with all the politeness, pretenses, and layers peeled off. So here's the scoop: At the University of California at Los Angeles, chimpanzees were given repeated opportunities to share banana rewards with other monkeys, but they simply wouldn't do it. Mind you, they didn't lose any of their own treat, but just had to press a button to release an extra banana down the chute to their buddy next door. These furry guys fully grasped the consequences of the button, but chose not to press it.

The study concluded that although they're social animals and sometimes show signs of cooperation with one another, chimps consistently refuse to show compassion to their fellow man, er. . .chimp. They remain indifferent and unsympathetic even if kindness costs them nothing.

In other words, they couldn't care less about others.

After confrontation with a NIB who must've escaped from that study, waxed his body, and found a pair of Dockers, I decided I just couldn't let agitation with annoying acquaintances make a monkey out of me. So I searched the Bible to see how Papa God instructs us to deal with difficult people. Grab your Bible and together let's explore:

- Matthew 5:44: Pray for them. Especially for their salvation. Want a shocker? You don't have to like someone to pray for them. But you may be surprised how bitterness evolves into something quite different when you're on your knees.
- James 5:16: Pray for healing in your rifted relationhip. Pray not that God will change them (that's up to Him), but that He'll let you see them through His eyes. The Rule of Five may help you see them the way their Creator does: Think of five positive things about your NIB before you allow yourself one negative thought. Not only will your effort to see them in a positive light make a difference in you, but their response to your subtle shift in attitude may surprise you.
- Proverbs 29:22: Defuse your anger. Release steam in a healthy way. Scream into your pillow. Whack the stuffing out of a ball (guess why I play tennis!). Pour out your anger in a long letter, then destroy it. Confide in a trusted friend, but take care not to fall into the trap of kindling your fire with her empathy.
- Leviticus 19:16: Resist the temptation to tell everyone about the injustice

you've suffered. Gossip (even rooted in truth) only ends in pain.

- Philippians 4:6–7: Relax. You don't *have* to win. Jesus has already won. The driving need to dominate every argument only results in loss: loss of respect, friendship, peace, and relationships. As my pastor, Mark Saunders, advises, "Choose to lose. Refuse to win."

- James 3:5: It's not necessarily bad to daydream about the snappy, movie-dialogue retorts that elude you during a confrontation, but *don't* follow through in real life. Make it a very limited engagement then delete that scathing-reply video playing in your head. It may feel cathartic while you're visualizing your clever, put-him-in-his-place monologue, but in time you'll feel a deeper satisfaction because you edited it out than if you'd played the scene live. Plus, you get two thumbs up from the Great Reviewer!

- Matthew 5:38–41: What would Jesus do? Cliché, maybe, but definitely applicable. Remember how He remained silent before His false accusers at His crucifixion trial (see Matthew 27:12–14)? Have you ever wondered if He was railing about injustice on the inside? You or I surely would have been. Regardless of how much inequity you've suffered, behave outwardly like Christ, pray for His power, and your inner emotions and thoughts will gradually transform to become more Christlike. Fake it at first if you have to—the *act* becomes *fact* as God changes you from the outside in.

- Psalm 37:8: Feeling anger is not sin; it's human. Acting on it is sin.

- Proverbs 3:5–6: Recognize that there's more going on than you can see. Only God knows what's truly in the NIB's heart and He's in control. It helps me to think of that NIB as a nut that's simply hard to crack. It's less stressful to deal with a Brazil nut than a tarantula in your batter.

- Proverbs 16:7: Respond, don't react. Take charge of your own attitude and actions. You can't control the NIB's, but you're responsible for yours.

- Hebrews 13:6: Do not let anxiety or fear dominate you.

- Romans 12:19–21: When you're ready to finally let go, imagine packing your anger into a box and watching the UPS truck drive it away. Give it to God and don't take it back. When revenge knocks on your heart's door, turn the dead bolt and picture the back bumper of that truck as it fades into the sunset. The anger is no longer yours. You've given it away to the One who will handle it for you. Let Him.

Girlfriend, unresolved conflict can definitely increase our feelings of anxiety and tension, which escalate over time. Like scum building up in the corners of the shower, emotional residue can dirty the edges of our peace without us even realizing it. As unsettling as it can be at the moment, it's important to deal with situations as they arise and not carry them around for weeks or even years like stinky loaded diapers.

Difficult people are often in our lives for unseen purposes. God's purposes. Perhaps to stretch us, grow us, or sand down our sharp edges by their friction.

Remember, even nutty lumps in the batter add flavor!

Assumptions are the termites of relationships.

HENRY WINKLER

LET'S DECOM-STRESS

1. What is our primary goal in dealing with difficult people according to Romans 12:17–18?

2. Who are the nuts in your batter? Are you more inclined to try to pulverize them or gently fold them in?

3. Do you ever relive a confrontation and come up with a dozen scripted Sandra Bullock retorts you wish you'd thought of? Don't worry—nearly everybody does that. Have you ever considered that maybe God gave us our initial deer-in-the-headlights response for a reason?

Family Heir-loons
—Creating Legacy—

*We will tell the next generation the
praiseworthy deeds of the L*ORD*, his power,
and the wonders he has done.*

PSALM 78:4 NIV

"I don't think *that woman* knows what she's talking about," Mama said with a haughty sniff.

"What woman?" I asked, more confused than usual. "There are no women here except you and me."

My eighty-one-year-old mother was surrounded on the seat of our minivan by the maps she toted everywhere. Chuck and I had offered to chauffeur my parents, both octogenarians, from their home in Florida to visit friends in Virginia. Although she was relegated to the backseat on our six-day road trip, Mama had assumed a strategic position from which to navigate her son-in-law driver over his right shoulder.

"*That woman* just doesn't know these back roads as well as I do." Mama's southern drawl was edged with resentment as she glared at our new female-voiced GPS monitor suction-cupped to the windshield. Mama had been at odds with *that woman* over every turn for the last four hundred miles. Heavy sigh.

Legacy, according to Webster, is something handed down from one who has gone before. That includes the good, the bad, and the loony. Sure, a few fishy traits swim in every gene pool, but there are some we'd really rather not dangle from our hooks in public.

Like the propensity for stating the obvious I inherited from my dad's mother, Granny Mitchell. Granny was a plump pigeon of a woman who was never seen in public without her signature crocheted tam perched atop tight gray curls. She had tams of every color in the catechism (isn't it coincidental that my family uses that same phrase about my perky little hats?). Granny was a boisterous, unfiltered version of Mayberry's Aunt Bee, southern accent and all.

One crisp fall evening while my sister and I were on an obligatory weekend visit to her tiny house in Georgia, Granny decided it would be great fun to take us, both in our early teens at the time, to a high school football game. Up until halftime, we managed, somehow, to live through the acute embarrassment of being escorted by our exuberant grandmother, dressed as uncool as one could possibly be in a floral church dress (and tam, of course).

But then the walls, they came a-tumblin' down.

As the marching band exited the gridiron, a stray dog wandered out to the fifty-yard line and proceeded to squat. Granny thought this was knee-slapping hilarious. As my sister and I desperately tried to ooze through the foot space beneath the bleachers, Granny stood in front of God and everybody, pointed her finger at the halftime spectacle, and announced to the entire east side of the stadium, "Look! There's a dog doing his business on the field! Bwa-ha-ha-ha!"

Although she's gone to her heavenly home now, certain keepsakes will always connect me with Granny. An engraved butterfly stickpin. Her hand-painted landscapes hanging on my wall. And her humongous glass mixing bowl, which brings her right into the kitchen with me every time I bake. I remember that bowl from my childhood as a comforting fixture in Granny's warm, love-filled kitchen. Now it graces mine. My daughter has already staked her claim on that bowl as a happy memento of her childhood as well.

Granny taught me the fine culinary art of Coca-Cola floats (in Georgia, it was never just "Coke"), foamy with vanilla ice cream and consumed with homemade doughnuts. We rolled canned biscuits out flat with a jelly jar, cut out center circles with cinnamon shaker lids, fried the dough in lard, then shook the marvels in a sack of confectioner's sugar until they were coated like thick snow. I, in turn, spent many giggly Friday family nights instructing these essential life skills to my kids.

Funny how so many of our legacies involve food, isn't it?

My family routinely ate dinner together as I was growing up, and when our children came along, Chuck and I habitually turned off the TV and gathered our brood face-to-face around the kitchen table at least once daily. What better method of communication? Of feeling the pulse of the family and forging lasting bonds?

We're not talking about good nutrition here. We're talking about intentionally making the time to instill values, family identity, and self-worth in our children. And maybe a few manners, too. If they don't learn these important, character-molding ideals from us, where will they learn them? Their friends? A reality show? The Internet?

Scary thought, isn't it? Worrying about negative influences on our children is a leading stress-producer for women, but it's such a relief to know there's something we can do about it.

A Columbia University study showed that teens who eat with their families five or more times weekly are less likely to smoke, drink, and hang out with sexually active friends. Joseph A. Califano Jr., chairman and president of the National Center on Addiction and Substance Abuse, puts it best: "Parental engagement is a critical weapon in the fight against substance abuse. If I could wave a wand, I'd make everyone have family dinners."

My synopsis? The family that chews together stays glued together.

And what fun family memories these little get-togethers create! I'll bet you, like me, have dozens. Like the time my toddler finger-painted spaghetti sauce all over her little self, her high chair, and the wall behind her. Or when preteen Matthew made a smart-aleck remark that boys were superior to girls in sports and got a glass of ice water poured over his head right there at the dinner table. By his, um, mother. That would be me. Okay, let's move on.

The point, of course, is that we pass on bits and pieces of ourselves to our children; these morsels, in turn, are passed on to countless future generations. We can't help the flat feet and connect-the-dots freckles they inherit, but we *can* intentionally transfer specific character-molding traits: dependency on God, the importance of prayer, loyalty, integrity, loving and protecting each other within the family.

The key is to ask ourselves: Am I living my faith out loud? Am I making it a priority to ensure that my legacy includes a living, breathing, dynamic relationship with my heavenly Father? It's never too late to lay the foundation for a strong and lasting faith dynasty!

Families are a lot like chocolate: sweet, flavorful, nutty, and may disrupt intestinal fortitude when internalized in large quantities.
DEBORA M. COTY

LET'S DECOM-STRESS

1. What are some of your favorite childhood memories with your parents and grandparents? What specific traits did you pick up from them?

2. According to Proverbs 8:19–21, when we share spiritual rather than material wealth with our loved ones, what fills their treasuries?

3. Name the three traits you desire more than anything else to pass on to your progeny.

Latitude for Gratitude
—LIVING GRATEFULLY—

*I will sing for joy at the
works of Your hands.*

PSALM 92:4 NASB

You won't hear any joyful songs from me today, Lord. Nope. Not a single note. A screech of frustration, maybe, or a wail of disappointment. How about nails on a chalkboard?

Here's the deal. It's my thirtieth wedding anniversary. I *should* be jubilant, rejoicing mightily at the works of Your hands. You were the magnet that brought Chuck and me together as bright-eyed college students, and the stitches that held our marriage together for three decades.

But, Papa God, Your man dropped the ball. It was his turn to plan our big celebration, since I masterminded a cross-country jaunt to see his favorite childhood band on our twentieth anniversary. Ironing out the details while keeping it a secret was a royal pain, but it was worth it all to see the delight on his face at the airport when I sprang the surprise.

You know the history, Lord. Since our twenty-fifth anniversary fell right after the 9/11 disaster, Chuck thought it best not to travel, so we deferred the European vacation plans (which I'd hatched, of course) to this year. I've been eagerly anticipating this trip for ten years. I dropped heavy hints that I was itching to go somewhere I'd never been and do something totally out of the ordinary. Something special—an experience the two of us could share and commemorate forever. I even requested a week off work to accommodate intercontinental travel.

I had such fun with my workmates, dreaming up possible destinations. Edinburgh would be lovely this time of year, or even London. I've always wanted

to explore Rome. But if not Europe, then at least Niagara Falls or the Grand Canyon. (Chuck leans toward frugality. Okay, he's just plain cheap.) That's okay. I yearn to see our own grand country from sea to shining sea!

So what exciting getaway did my darling spouse plan? A weekend at the beach an hour away from home. We live in Florida, for crying out loud! We're up to our eyeballs in water and sand! What is wrong with this man You gave me, Lord?

I had to cancel my days off and slink back to work with my tail between my legs as everyone bombarded me with, "Where did you go?" "Why are you back so soon?"

"Did he surprise you with a weekend in Paris?" "A Broadway show in New York?"

So here I sit, simmering with resentment as my friend Sue e-mails that she and her husband are flying to Barcelona for a thirtieth anniversary Mediterranean cruise, and Janis reminds me that her husband—on his own initiative—planned a Jamaican holiday for their twenty-fifth. And then Cynthia requests prayer for their upcoming anniversary tour of Washington, DC. Arggh!

Could there possibly be any more salt to grind into my gaping wound?

What's that? Did You say something, Lord?

No, I guess I wouldn't want Cynthia's husband. Or Janis's or Sue's. Well, maybe Sue's. No, you're right, Father, I wouldn't swap husbands with them for all the exotic vacations in the world. But why can't my husband be more in tune with my needs and desires, more eager to give me the *good* things, to shower me with love, adoration, and undivided attention?

That's weird, Papa God. It sounded like You said, "Because that's *My* job."

You did? Oh. Well. Let me marinate on that a minute. Say what? Yeah, yeah, I hear You, Father: Give the man a little latitude. He's only human. He has limitations.

Oh, Lord-a-mercy, You can say *that* again.

Gratitude? You want me to be grateful? For what? Okay, okay, I'm thinking. Well, he *did* spend a lot of time searching for the most adorable B&B in our area. And at least he had the foresight to make dinner reservations at that nice little bistro. And when we got caught in the rainstorm and my rented bicycle handle streaked rust stains across my new white blouse, he spent three hours scrubbing with every stain remover on the planet until he got it out.

All points for him, I'll concede, but his score's still in the single digits.

You say You want me to work on living thankfully? Hmm. As much as I hate to admit it, I suppose that's a good idea, Father.

In fact, I just read about university research concluding that those who are grateful on a regular basis are healthier mentally and physically. It's like going to the gym—you can't go just once a year and expect to benefit; you've got to make it a habit. Living gratefully doesn't come naturally—it's a discipline we have to consider important enough to adopt. Like having a daily quiet time or flossing our teeth.

I find it amazing that studies actually prove thankful people are less envious and resentful. Grateful people sleep better, are physically more active, and have lower blood pressure. Guess I could stand a little more of that, huh, Lord? You really don't have to poke me with Your elbow. . .I get it. There are perks to a lifestyle of gratitude. After all, I can't be depressed and thankful at the same time.

Well, as far as this man You picked out for me, maybe actions do speak louder than nerds. What I mean is, I know he loves me by the little things he does. So maybe a few not-so-little things can slide by forgiven. And forgotten.

You're right, Father—maybe I shouldn't forget everything. Some things need remembering. Like that brand-new computer monitor he gave me for my birthday last November. I didn't want a computer monitor. I wanted a ski trip. I was so ungrateful (*what* was I thinking?) that the poor man tried to return it to the store. When the store refused to take it back, Chuck rewrapped it in pretty gift paper, added a big red bow, and lo and behold, the thing reappeared beneath my Christmas tree. Talk about regifting! We laughed ourselves silly and I ended up loving it. Go figure.

Maybe I *will* sing for joy after all. And look for something to be grateful for every single day. And brush up on my French for my turn to plan his amazing thirty-first anniversary surprise!

Even when I have pains,
I don't have to be one.

MAYA ANGELOU

LET'S DECOM-STRESS

1. Can you think of five things to be grateful for this very minute?

2. Is there someone in your life who drives you to utter an ongoing prayer for a grateful attitude? What is it about him or her that drives you bonkers? What about the person is a blessing? C'mon now, dig deep!

3. Colossians 2:7 advises us, "Let your lives be built on him. . . and you will overflow with thankfulness" (NLT). What steps can you take to make living thankfully an everyday habit?

Chic Chat

—Nurturing Girlfriends—

Someone might be able to beat up
one of you, but not both of you.

Ecclesiastes 4:12 cev

Didn't your heart bleed for astronaut Heidemarie Stefanyshyn-Piper when she lost her purse while space-walking on international television a few years ago?

Actually, it was her tool bag and it wasn't her fault—a grease gun exploded while she was lubing a solar panel. As she busily cleaned up the mess, the bag slipped from her gloved hand and the entire world watched her white intergalactic pocketbook float away to no doubt grace the closet of some stylish lady Martian.

My guess is that men watching the newscast just shrugged and flipped the channel to a ball game, but I'll bet I'm not the only woman who totally identified with the mortification of this space sister. I can't count on three feet the number of purses I've lost.

There are some things only women can understand. Like why unannounced guests can be stressful. Or how come you grab your cell phone to answer the question when a bumper sticker asks, How's my driving? Call 1-800-. . . Or how to read your child's temperature by his eyes. That it's absolutely necessary to own four pairs of black shoes. Or that your dog needs a hug instead of a swat when he watches you pet the cat and then reappears two minutes later with your favorite ceramic statue in his mouth.

And, of course, there's the BBP. You know—the bursting bladder phenomenon. That inexplicable law of nature that expands one six-ounce cup of hot tea consumed before bedtime into two quarts an hour after you hit the sack. And then mysteriously dredges up another quart every half hour thereafter. The gift that keeps on giving all night long.

Girls bond over such dribble, er, I mean drivel. Yes, girlfriends fill in the holes in our relationships with others. . .especially the sinkholes. Girlfriends make us laugh when we least expect it. I adore an e-mail I received from my Hispanic friend Nina (who writes in the same accent with which she speaks) about her contribution to an upcoming girlfriend brunch: "I have at hand some yougart and whipped cream, walnuts, and a little fruit. I can make a concussion with that."

There's no one on earth with whom I'd rather share a yougart concussion.

Girlfriends are the way we hone our Christlikeness. Face it, there are no perfect friends. If we wait until we find one before investing ourselves, we'll be lonely forever. By spending time together, we learn how to be there for others, to be nurturing, loving, and nonjudgmental. We practice extending forgiveness and compassion, just as our Godfriend does when we spend time with Him.

We develop patience in these give-and-take relationships with select girls who are true *friends*, not just those with whom we are being friendly. We give them our attention, allegiance, and trust. In return we receive affirmation, security, and honest advice. Valuable advice from someone who desires a solution to our problems as much as we do. "A man's counsel is sweet to his friend" (Proverbs 27:9 NASB).

But what happens when we neglect those special girlfriendships? When we get so busy or distracted that we take them for granted and cease making time for them?

Have you ever seen an overgrown garden? A once beautiful, well-tended, manicured landscape that has grown ugly with tangled vines and choking weeds? The lovely place that once lit eyes with gladness begins to turn them away in repulsion. All because of inattention. Lack of investment. Indifference.

So how do we find time to nurture girlfriendships so they don't become like neglected gardens? To maintain that unique relationship in which we can un-frazzle by baring our kaput nerves and distressed souls? To be the friend that our friend needs so that we know we'll always have each other's backs?

❧ Make girlfriend time a priority. Consider this time crucial to your sanity.
❧ Invest yourself. Plan ahead to make time for this lifetime relationship.
❧ Do life together. Schedule chic-chat time—weekly, if possible, or at least

every other week. Be creative in rooting out opportunities to rendezvous: shop together (you've got to do it anyway, right?), meet for lunch or lattes, carpool to events together, arrange kids' playdates, or volunteer for the same school, church, or community events.

- Grow together. Combine spiritual and emotional nurturing. Join forces in a Bible study or prayer group. Be accountability partners. Keep prayer journals and share God's amazing grace notes in your life with each other.

- Send pal-entines. And I don't mean red hearts on February 14. Let her know you're thinking about her and praying for her during the week by personal e-mails (not just forwards!), notes, or quick calls. Add these important gal-pal tune-ups to your calendar so you won't forget.

- Celebrate together. For anything and everything. Cheer, inflate balloons, hug, wear tiaras, bake cakes. . .uplift your hearts in acknowledgment of every victory, however big or small. Life's made up of little accomplishments— don't obsess over the holes and miss the doughnuts!

- Hold hands through the tough times. Physically, sure, but emotionally, too. No one else can support like a girlfriend. She needs you. You need her. In totally inexpressible ways. Nurture your relationship to a level deeper than words.

I will never forget how my girlfriend Cheryl ministered to me when I was sidelined by a skiing accident that required three surgeries on my left knee within seven months. For the first few months, kind church folk brought food, prayers were lifted up, and get well cards arrived. Despite my crutches, braces, chronic pain, and inability to get around, I was fine, just fine, I assured everyone.

But Cheryl tuned in to my depressed spirit carefully tucked beneath a smiling exterior. Every second or third day, month after month, I received a three-minute phone call simply inquiring, "How *are* you today?"

Some days I burst into tears when I heard her voice; other days we chatted about inane life happenings. But always, her faithful, assuring "Just wanted you to know I was thinking about you" healed me more thoroughly than any medical treatment ever could.

I was, in turn, blessed to reciprocate when my friend Sharon was diagnosed with cancer. Through months of tests, chemo, surgery, and recovery, I made it a point to devote a few minutes every other day to a brief call. She says those faithful little reminders that someone cared meant more to her than pure gold.

Never forget that the best stress reliever we have is each other! God blessed us gals with a unique kinship that helps us grasp underlying meanings. Like the dear sister at one of my speaking events of whom I asked, "Do you think the way I do this is tacky?" Without missing a beat, she picked up that I needed a little affirmation, flashed me a sly smile, raised one feisty eyebrow, and replied, "Hey, you're the one who made tacky okay!"

I sense a new girlfriend in the making!

> Friends are those rare people who ask how
> you are and then wait for the answer.
>
> UNKNOWN

LET'S DECOM-STRESS

1. Romans 12:15 says, "Laugh with your happy friends when they're happy; share tears when they're down" (MSG). Do you have a girlfriend who fulfills this verse in your life?

2. Are you this kind of friend to someone? Who?

3. What are you and your girlfriend(s) currently doing to grow together spiritually and emotionally? Is this something you'd like to take to the next level?

Ah, Sweet Sistah-hood!
—SIBLINGS—

Love wisdom like a sister.

PROVERBS 7:4 NLT

I was bigger and badder (in every sense of the word) than my sister, Cindy, from the time we started elementary school, though I was two years younger. A rough-and-tumble tomboy, I was the son Daddy never had. Cindy was a girly girl. She liked to loll about painting her toenails; I wanted to wrestle. She adored shopping; I'd rather stick hot needles in my eyes. Her preference for playing was jacks; mine was swatting anything with a stick.

Including Cindy.

Torture was my favorite sister game. One of my earliest memories is of the two of us in the bathtub as preschoolers. I recall marveling at the perfect crimson imprint of my chubby little hand on Cindy's bare, pale back after I'd whacked her just to see if she'd cry.

Without other siblings in the playmate pool, Cindy was my captive audience. In order to coerce her into hop-scotching, pogo-sticking, or tossing a softball with me in the backyard, I resorted to threatening imminent death, or worse, taunting her with the surefire sister-mover: "Fatty-fatty-two-by-four, can't fit through the bathroom door!" She was the width of a licorice stick, but that was irrelevant.

Our nightly ritual in the bedroom we shared was tapping messages to each other in the dark for hours after we were forbidden to talk. We communicated by a syllable-based quasi-Morse code. For example, five taps = see-you-to-mor-row; four taps = g'wan-to-sleep-now (drawling *going* into one syllable is a southern talent); three taps = I-love-you; two hurried taps followed by a dive under the covers at the brisk sound of Mama's approaching footsteps = look out!

One warm summer afternoon when the neighborhood kids were killing time before supper, we launched a rousing game of chase in our yard. Fifth-grade Cindy, in a stylish wraparound skirt, was the only one not in raggedy cutoff jeans. (She was trying to impress Michael from next door with her mature femininity.) Since many of our neighbors were boys, when I was "it," I made a beeline straight for Cindy. She was the only one I knew I could catch, and who wanted yucky boy cooties anyway?

As I lunged for Cindy's fleeing form, my outstretched fingers snagged the fabric bow tying the two ends of her skirt together. As she ran away, her wraparound dramatically unwrapped, leaving the rest of us howling and clutching our sides as she bolted into the house, screaming hysterically in her lacy white panties.

I made it up to her the following summer when I climbed the ladder out of the packed community pool and turned to find Cindy emerging behind me, unaware that her bathing suit top was hanging completely off. Thoughtful and sensitive sister that I was, I stuck my foot in her face and shoved her back underwater.

You know, I don't think she ever thanked me properly for that.

One fateful afternoon when I was ten, I remember sitting astraddle Cindy after having wrestled her to the floor of our bedroom. On the cold terrazzo floor, I pinned her hands above her head as I dangled my stringy hair in her face. Sputtering and spewing, she yelled for Mama to come to her rescue as she had countless times before.

Before actually spotting her in the doorway, I *felt* Mama's all-powerful presence, arms crossed, head shaking slowly. In a flash, I saw my delinquent young life pass before my eyes and steeled myself for the gathering hurricane.

To my utter amazement, Mama's voice was low and controlled and not directed to me at all. "Cindy, if you can't defend yourself against your little sister, then you deserve what you get." And she disappeared.

Glory hallelujah! It was D-Day for me!

As teenagers, I was usually thrust into the big sister role. I suppose it was because I was larger, louder, and perhaps a smidge meaner. Pretty and vivacious, Cindy often garnered unwanted attention from boys in high school. She wheedled

me into breaking the news that she couldn't (truthfully, she *wouldn't!*) go out with them and even convinced Mama that I should tag along on dates she couldn't tactfully avoid.

Feeling like a half-bouncer, half-chaperone, I did *not* want to be there (and you can be assured the date felt the same way!) but at least I got a free movie or bowling out of it. I amused myself by echoing Linus from Charles Shulz's *Peanuts* comic: "Big sisters are the crab grass in the lawn of life."

Siblings are the reluctant instructors in our life classrooms. They're our crash dummies, our failed experiments; the unfortunate people we practice on to learn how *not* to treat others. They unwittingly teach us civility by being the ones who suffer the consequences of our mistakes as we learn the virtues of kindness, compassion, fairness, forgiveness, and helping one another.

Yet despite trampled feelings, bruises, and occasional concussions, there are no more loyal companions than siblings. We're roses and tulips from the same garden! What would we do without them? They're as much a part of our DNA as our crooked noses. We love them, admire them, and are irritated senseless by them all at the same time.

We see their faults all too well (and don't mind pointing them out a'tall), but we're willing to overlook petty grievances and love them unconditionally anyway. We share memories no one else in the world knows about, and they understand where we're coming from better than even our spouses.

After all, our brothers and sisters are passengers in our lifeboat, and it would be suicidal to try to blow them out of the water. So we might as well accept them as heaven-sent companions for this voyage of life and try to paddle in sync.

Besides, it just isn't the same without them—like a missing piece in the puzzle of our lives. You don't realize how important that piece is until it's gone.

When Cindy left for college, I thought I'd enjoy the peace and absence of conflict, but I was stunned to discover how much I missed her. She left a gap that no one else could fill. In the movie *In Her Shoes*, Rose Feller (played by Toni Collette) voiced every sister's sentiments when she was trying to explain the unexplainable bond she shared with her incorrigible sister, Maggie (played by Cameron Diaz): "Without her. . .I don't make sense."

No, without our siblings, we just don't make sense.

Cindy and I grew closer over the years, and now through a series of miracles, we're blessed to grow old together on the same block. Only she's my antiaging serum in human form; when we're snickering together, I feel twelve again. Although I seldom pin her to the ground anymore or leave my paw prints on her back, I daresay she wouldn't dare wear a wraparound near me even today (some things never change!). Even without torture, she's always there for me. . .overlooking my quirks, helping me tread water on tsunami days, providing insight when the relatives get gorky, finding balance when my world is all off kilter.

Her resounding laugh alone detangles my mind cramps and takes me back to a simpler, less stressful time when all I had to worry about were ant bites, Pixy Stix, and staying in the tub long enough to bathe the important parts.

*A sister shares childhood memories
and grown-up dreams.*

UNKNOWN

LET'S DECOM-STRESS

1. What's your fondest childhood memory of each of your siblings?

2. Which of your siblings were your crash dummies? Whose crash dummy were you? What life lessons did you learn from your sibling experiences?

3. According to Proverbs 18:19, "A brother wronged is more unyielding than a fortified city" (NIV). Is there an unresolved riftbetween you and your sibling? What's preventing you from starting the mending process today?

Teddies to Toasters
—Marital Intimacy—

Marriage should be honored by all.
Hebrews 13:4 NIV

Twenty-year-old Claire tells the story of her family going on a cruise to celebrate her grandparents' sixtieth wedding anniversary. Grandma and Grandpa, both in their eighties, were chosen as contestants for the "Oldie-Wed Show." Grandpa's answer to the question, "Where was the craziest place you ever made love to your wife?" was, after a few moments of concentrated thought, "A barn."

When Grandma was brought onstage and asked the same question, she immediately replied, "A train car."

"Oh!" Grandpa colored slightly. "She's right."

On the way back to their cabin, Grandma gently rebuked her husband. "Honey, you shouldn't have missed that answer. Don't you remember how wild and crazy we were rolling around on that train to Paris?" They giggled like schoolchildren.

"Paris?" Claire interrupted. "Didn't you two just go to Europe six months ago?"

"That's right!" Grandma answered with a wink.

Ah, love, sweet love. It's what the world needs now. And tomorrow. And decades from now. I crack up every time I recall my friend's account of her husband misquoting the famous Jerry McGuire line in a hot and heavy romantic moment. Instead of passionately whispering, "You complete me," he murmured, "You finish me."

Without missing a beat, she replied, "Not yet, but I'm still trying."

We love them to pieces but they drive us batty. Men. Why do so many stressful things that happen to women start with that word? *Men*struation, *men*opause, *men*tal anguish, *mén*age (French for "housekeeping"). . .even *men*ace. A physician friend told me about a man who came into the emergency room with five gunshot wounds. *Five!* The doctor met the patient's wife in the waiting room. "Mrs. Jones, I'm sorry to tell you that your husband's been shot."

"I know," she replied with remarkable calmness. "I'm the one who shot him." She slowly shook her head. "Day after day I wash all those clothes and he won't help fold a single one."

Yep, we gals have the potential to evolve into real menaces. It seems to me that a lot of marital strain could be avoided if men clued in to those three little words that women long to hear from their husbands: *Can I help?*

My Chuck actually has a good handle on this concept. Last Valentine's Day when my wicked pooch Fenway polished off the platter of heart-shaped brownies I'd baked and hidden in my closet, he hocked up a muddy, chunky backwash all over the bedroom rug. Chuck heroically sopped up the whole mess. With my best pink towels. Eww.

In terms men understand, marriage isn't a spectator sport. We're in this game together, and it takes teamwork to post a winning season. Intimacy in the bedroom (touchdown!) will happen a whole lot faster when all the players do their part to move the ball down the field. . . getting the household fed, washed, de-cluttered, and prepared for tomorrow. The quarterback can't do it alone. She needs a big strong running back to advance the ball and move her into scoring position.

Husbands don't always realize that it's the small plays that drive wives either toward or away from the end zone. Once when I was running out the door, late to a big speaking event, Chuck remarked, "You're not going to wear your hair like *that*, are you?"

Whistle. Thirty-yard penalty.

And then there was the time when, after napping in the car, I arrived for a TV interview with a shock of hair sticking straight out the back of my head like a rooster tail and Chuck never made a peep. "I thought you meant for it to look like that," he later defended himself as I died a thousand deaths while viewing the broadcast. (You can still view a clip of my hairdo-doo on my website, www. DeboraCoty.com.)

Or the "way cool" bathroom scale birthday gift he bought me that measured not just weight but body fat, too. "How could anybody not love this?" he wondered when I didn't.

But then there are the play-of-the-week victories. Like the time I had three surgeries on the same knee within seven months and Chuck took me to a Valentine's Day dance on crutches just to cheer me up. The three of us—Chuck, moi, and our shared crutch—huddled on the dance floor to the romantic strains of "You Are So Beautiful."

Score!

We gals love to hear about other marital teams' winning seasons, too. Like the Valentine's Day on which my friend Rhonda felt utterly repulsive with an allergy-induced swollen, red, runny nose. Then a flock of robins flew overhead while her husband was working in the yard and deposited freshly digested berries on his head. Despite the setbacks, terms of endearment like "Poopy Head" and "Snot Nose" resulted in a romantic evening together.

My friend Mary once witnessed a husband at the Cancer Center pushing his wife's wheelchair as she sadly fingered an enormous bandage on her neck. As the elevator doors opened on the ninth floor, Mary and her family hesitated to enter, noticing the woman's downcast countenance. "Do you mind if we share the elevator with you?" Mary asked the couple.

"Not if you sing us a Christmas carol," the man replied, glancing down at his disheartened wife. "They're her favorites." Although it was June, that elevator resounded with the uplifting strains of "Joy to the World" as smiling faces, including the one in the wheelchair, emerged on the ground floor.

It helped me understand my man better and dramatically reduced expectation stress once I realized that men are a lot like, well, like dogs. Now, don't get me wrong—I love dogs. This is not male bashing. It's just that men have simple basic needs: someone to feed them, play with them, scratch where it itches, pat them on the head, and gush "Good boy!" now and then. They need, above all, respect. They thrive with acknowledgment of their strength, courage, and hunting skills—their admirable ability to provide for their loved ones. There's a lot less growling and a lot more tail wagging when these basic needs are met. And they truly aspire to become woman's best friend.

Then their little quirks don't seem so, well, quirksome. Like when Chuck rolls out of bed at midnight to rearrange the stuffed animals on my dresser because he can't sleep with that scary bunny staring at him. Or when he's driving along in the car, listening to the Bible on CD, and runs plum off the road when the soundtrack suddenly explodes with swine squeals as Jesus casts the demons into the herd of pigs.

Face it, we're different. Men are rock concerts. Women are symphonies. We may approach the beat differently but we can both still enjoy music.

I try to remember that I really have two husbands: Chuck and Jesus. As a believer, part of the bride of Christ, I am married to Him as well (see Ephesians 5:25–27; Revelation 21:9). *Ishi,* the Hebrew name for God used in Hosea 2:16, translates "husband." The Lover of our soul assumes the traditional husband's role as protector, provider, and faithful companion. Only He will never leave us or forsake us—He refuses to divorce us no matter how unfaithful we are.

What a revelation when we view our wifely role from that perspective! We begin to see our mates through the same compassionate, forgiving, unconditional eyes with which Christ sees us. Our husband's desires become important to us. We *want* to meet his needs.

And amazingly those touchdown victory dances become oh, so sweet!

God created man, but I could do better.

Erma Bombeck

LET'S DECOM-STRESS

1. Grab your Bible and look up Paul's comparison of marriage to Christ's relationship to His church in Ephesians 5:25–33. I love how verse 32 calls it "a profound mystery" (NIV). So true, isn't it? Thankfully, we don't have to understand how sacrificial love works for us to enjoy its benefits.

2. If you're married, name three things you love about your husband. Now name three things you think he adores about you. How willing are you to freely give these things to him? Are there ever strings attached? How does this arrangement compare to Jesus' sacrificial love for us?

3. Consider a couple that you feel has an intimate marriage. What factors do you think contribute to that husband and wife's closeness? Are there particular aspects of their relationship that you'd like to emulate in yours?

Pacifiers to Puberty
—MOTHERING—

*The troubles of my heart are
enlarged; bring me out of my distresses.*
PSALM 25:17 NASB

My friend Debbie was a mother of eight, including ten-month-old twins, when she and her husband, Rich, were faced with a move out of state. They put their house on the sluggish market and prayed.

No one showed up for the first three realtor-generated appointments. Each time, Debbie had scoured bathrooms, mopped floors, stowed dirty clothes, tidied toys, and even baked cookies minutes before scheduled arrivals for that homey, "You'll want to live here!" motif. Then, at the last minute, she'd whisked the kids over to visit a friend to avoid their normal chaotic household atmosphere that boldly declared, "He who steps through this door is dead meat."

On the fourth try, ever-optimistic Debbie kept the squirming kids at bay for twenty minutes in a single room at a neighbor's house, but when Rich and the real estate agent phoned with another apparent no-show, she trooped them home for lunch. The kids swarmed the house like ravenous locusts and began their usual onslaught of devastation and destruction.

Amid stray globs of peanut butter and squashed ravioli sabotaging the linoleum, the six-year-old threw up his Chef Boyardee and the grinning toddler presented Debbie with an especially smelly diaper. So much for fresh cookie ambience!

At that moment, the potential buyers pulled up, a quiet young couple with one immaculate child.

Debbie threw a handful of cinnamon sticks on the stove to boil in a feeble attempt to mask the nauseating conglomeration of offensive odors while Rich flew out the back door with the stinky diaper. So why did it still reek like a skunk had expired behind the refrigerator? Oh no! The twins had each dirtied their diapers, too!

While Debbie scrubbed strained peas off little faces, billows of black, acrid smoke began permeating the room. Yikes! The water had boiled out and the cinnamon scorched.

With one poopy baby under each arm, Rich hurdled over piles of soiled clothing as Debbie frantically sliced onions and garlic into a sauté pan of melting butter. And shot heavenward a prayer that the buyers were Italian!

Heavy sigh. It would be nice to think parenting actually gets easier when kids grow older. 'Tis but a pipe dream.

Laura, my friend who's a single mother of two teens, cut a deal with her reluctant daughters: they'd cook while she cleaned up afterward, or vice versa. After a few *whatever*s accompanied by eyeball rolls, they chose the latter. Everything went fine for the first week, but then the girls developed that dreaded teenage malady, DAM: disorder of adolescent memory. Amazing how stacks of dirty dishes are so easy to forget!

There are times you just want to hook a voltmeter up to their little punkin brains to see if *anything* is getting through.

After encountering the third sinkful of crusty plates and greasy pizza pans, Laura devised an ingenious plan to solve the problem without uttering a single syllable. That evening, she simply forgot to fix dinner. When the girls groused long and loud, Laura opened a can of Alpo, fried it up in a skillet, and served it to her astounded offspring on paper plates.

No more leaning towers of pizza. The DAM had burst.

Yep, ulcer is *kids* spelled backward. Well, it should be anyway. The parent handbook should inform us of the risks before we swim upstream and spawn. Having a kid is like getting your tongue pierced—you're committed. Nothing will be the same from now on. That single act will affect every waking moment of your existence. And some non-waking moments, too.

I have recurring nightmares about the time I loaded my homemade chocolate layer cake onto the car backseat floorboard so it would be safe from the grasp

of my two preschoolers en route to the church banquet. Five-year-old Matthew climbed aboard and buckled himself into his booster seat as I strapped toddler Cricket into her car seat on the other side of the car. Arriving at church, I opened Matthew's car door and reached in to unbuckle his seat belt when I noticed that his right sneaker was caked with mud. Mud that smelled suspiciously delicious. I glanced down to find a perfect size-five imprint in the fudge frosting of my gorgeous cake.

And then there was the time darling little Matthew appeared in the middle of our dinner party in nothing but his Spiderman underpants and dozens of my Kotex stuck to every square inch of his little body.

Or years later when both my college-age kids were vacationing with us and a horrified yowl resounded from our motel bathroom at 7:00 a.m. Matthew had groggily begun brushing his teeth when he realized that the foul-tasting toothpaste he'd liberally applied to his toothbrush was his sister's yeast infection cream.

And then there are those moments when we, like the mother of Jesus, treasure the special memories and keep them close to ponder in our hearts (see Luke 2:19).

During the chaos of a move shortly after she'd received a diagnosis of cancer, my devastated friend Kim was sitting in her closet, surrounded by half-filled cardboard boxes. She just couldn't go on. Shoving a box with her foot, she inadvertently uncovered a forgotten bag of hidden Hershey's Kisses.

If she'd ever needed kisses from heaven, it was now.

As she consumed the candies one after the other, Kim's ten-year-old son appeared in the doorway. He eyed the growing mound of crinkly silver foil and gazed at his mother's tearstained face. Without saying a word, he sat down on the closet floor and began peeling chocolates for her.

If that doesn't light your fire, girlfriend, the wood's wet.

My best motherhood stress reliever has been to remind myself in the midst of the fray that the most important things in my world are my people. *My peeps.* Those beautiful souls God has entrusted to my care for a few short years. They require and deserve the best of my attention even as my day is constantly interrupted with their blessings.

"Don't you see that children are GOD's best gift?" (Psalm 127:3 MSG). Did you catch that, fellow frazzled mom? God's very *best* gift is our children.

If we can just keep grasping that elusive reassurance even as our groping fingernails cling to the last shreds of maternal sanity, by God's grace our children won't one day echo my disillusioned friend who sadly admitted, "My mother was merely the vessel that carried me for nine months. Nothing more."

An ounce of mother is
worth a pound of clergy.

SPANISH PROVERB

LET'S DECOM-STRESS

1. If you're a mom, what's your craziest maternal memory of your kids?

2. In what way does your faith make a difference in your responses to daily family catastrophes?

3. Pause to reflect on a time when you, like Mary in Luke 2:19, were so moved that you treasured the moment and stored it in your heart.

Minding My Earth Suit
—PHYSICAL MAINTENANCE—

We are the temple of the living God.
2 CORINTHIANS 6:16 NIV

One of the most important and long-lasting relationships we must cultivate is with these earth suits God has entrusted to us for a limited time. Depending upon the condition in which we maintain them, our bodies can be warmly comforting, a source of pleasure, a vehicle for adventure, or a painfully restrictive straitjacket.

The Bible says our bodies are God's temples. If we, as temple caretakers, are to withstand battering gales and the onslaught of relentless enemy attacks, we must fortify our living structures from within! Knowledge and prevention of the forces assaulting our temple edifices are our best defense.

As an occupational therapist specializing in upper extremity rehabilitation for over thirty years, I've found that women are especially vulnerable to specific maladies related to a stressful lifestyle. I'm going to put on my professional hat now and share valuable medical information that you would pay hundreds of dollars for in a rehabilitation therapy clinic. Ready to get a bit technical?

You may be acquainted with a rather common overuse syndrome, or repetitive strain injury (RSI) as it's sometimes called, known as carpal tunnel syndrome (CTS). CTS occurs when the median nerve is pinched at the wrist by chronically poor positioning or internal inflammation due to constant finger or wrist motion (such as in typing or repetitive gripping or pinching). The median nerve innervates the thumb, index finger, long finger, and half the ring finger. Numbness and tingling (called *paresthesias*) or pain from CTS can occur in any or all of these digits. Symptoms are often worse at night or early morning because of our tendency to sleep with our wrists flexed (in a modified fetal position), thus impinging the nerve. Picture yourself bending a straw, thus cutting off the flow inside. That's what happens to the quarter-sized tunnel containing tendons, an artery, and the median nerve when you keep your wrist bent.

Treatment by an orthopedic physician should be pursued immediately upon onset of symptoms; the earlier treatment begins, the better the chances of avoiding surgery. Frequent rest breaks and stretching of the flexor muscles (assume a praying hands position palm-to-palm at chin level, then lower the hands to your waist, spreading your elbows and keeping the palms together), plus use of wrist support splints to keep the tunnel open at night and during daily heavy hand activity, are highly recommended. Your MD or therapist may show you a median nerve glide exercise that can release nerve tension.

Another common overuse ailment is *tennis elbow* (lateral epicondylitis), evidenced by pain in the dorsum (outside) of the elbow. Tennis elbow is basically tendonitis of the muscles that extend the wrist and fingers and is usually caused by repetitive reaching (for example, operating a computer mouse farther than fifteen inches from your waist), lifting with the arm extended (as in carrying a heavy purse or grocery bag), or cocking back the wrist (like a tennis player getting ready to hit a ball—hence the term *tennis elbow*).

Cortisone shots or iontophoresis (something therapists do with a little electrical machine to introduce tissue-calming steroids to the painful area without an actual injection), icing (I'm talking ice here, not cream cheese frosting), and wearing a tennis elbow cuff (to reduce muscle friction in the upper forearm) can reduce pain, but to keep it away for good, frequent extensor muscle stretching is a must. To do this, use your opposite hand to gently bend the wrist forward with the elbow extended. It may twang at first, but your body will grow to crave such stretching that loosens the tight muscles.

Golfers elbow (medial epicondylitis) is a similar tendonitis condition of the muscles that flex the hand and wrist. Too much gripping, pinching, or curling the wrist forward can produce pain at the inside of the elbow (the pinky finger side when your hand is facing you) where the flexor muscles originate.

Treatment includes anti-inflammatory meds, frequent rest breaks from gripping activities, and stretching the flexor muscles by placing the palm against a wall and straightening your elbow. The praying hands exercise previously described helps also.

Another common RSI, *DeQuervain's tenosynovitis*, frequently occurs in women when the thumb performs repetitive movements, creating friction and inflammation in the narrow compartment at the base of the thumb through which two key tendons glide. Burning pain is common on the thumb side of the wrist. I often see DeQuervain's in gals over forty when decades of twisting, turning, chopping, and slicing on behalf of their families takes a toll. Dentists, hygienists, and hairstylists tend to struggle with it, too.

Treatment usually consists of anti-inflammatory meds, cortisone (some physicians don't give cortisone injections at this location because permanent discoloration may occur), and use of a thumb spica immobilization splint. DeQuervain's is sometimes mistaken for arthritis of the carpometacarpal (CMC) joint at the base of the thumb (another common malady of middle-aged women). Your orthopedic MD can discern the difference.

As with all RSIs, rest and altering the motions that caused the problem are the keys to decreasing symptoms. We *must* listen to our bodies when they tell us via pain, "Hey, I can't do this any longer!"

Girls, Papa God didn't intend for our bodies to stay in the same positions hour after hour or to perform the same functions repeatedly without resting. Paced daily time-outs for a few simple stretching exercises (which you can even do in a desk chair or car) can bring immense relief to painful necks and tight shoulders:

- Exaggerated shoulder rolls: Forward ten times and then ten times backward.
- Ear-to-shoulder stretches: Gently push the head toward each shoulder with the opposite hand. Hold ten seconds. Note: It's important to completely relax your neck muscles and move the head with your hand for this and the following two exercises; contracted muscles don't stretch well!
- Chin-to-shoulder stretches: Use the opposite hand to rotate the chin toward each shoulder. Hold ten seconds.
- Chin tucks: Using your hand to push the chin down and back toward the Adam's apple relieves tension in the muscles at the base of the skull. . . . Bye-bye, tension headache!
- "Chicken necks": Thrust the chin forward. Hold five seconds.
- Pectoralis stretches: Clasp hands behind the back and lift, squeezing the

scapula (shoulder blades) together. Hold ten seconds.

If you're at home and have a little more room to move, lie on your back on the floor or a firm bed and try these awesome full-body stretches:

- Chest stretches: Place a rolled beach towel in line with your spine from the base of your neck to your bum. Now spread your arms outward into a T position, take some deep breaths, and hold for one minute. Repeat in a Y position to stretch different muscle fibers.
- Trunk extension: Place the rolled beach towel under your upper back perpendicular to your spine and extend your arms overhead. Allow yourself to melt into the towel roll. Hold this tension-relieving arch one minute; repeat with the roll beneath your middle back, then your lower back. Can you say ahhhhh?

Okay, let's get back to the essential basics: breathing. According to Dr. Nick Hall in *Winning the Stress Challenge*, controlled, deep breathing is crucial in stress management. When we're acutely frazzled, we often react with quick, shallow breathing that can result in vascular changes, dizziness, and even more stress. Breathing affects your blood gases, which alter your heart rate and muscle tension throughout your entire body.

Dr. Hall advises, "Simply drawing three long, deep breaths—inhaling through the nose, filling the lungs, distending the diaphragm, and then exhaling slowly through the mouth—has a substantial effect on altering the chemical makeup of the blood, and therefore, on alleviating fear or anxiety." Deep breathing also acts as a sort of air conditioner for the brain, cooling down cognitive heat waves and downshifting you to a more relaxed state.

Let's admit it—none of us want our temples to fall into ruins. With a sturdy foundation of prevention and a slap or two of maintenance mortar, our flesh-and-blood cathedrals can glorify God for decades to come without one brick crumbling from neglect.

For fast-acting relief, try slowing down.

LILY TOMLIN

Let's Decom-stress

1. Considering that your body is a temple of God, would you say that your edifice is currently in need of repairs or renovation? Which parts?

2. Take a few minutes to try each of the stretches recommended above. Which seems to work best for what ails you? (Hint: Self-massaging the upper shoulder and neck muscles for even twenty seconds will do wonders for you, too.) Will you commit to two-minute stretch breaks every few hours during the day? C'mon, sister, do it for *you*!

3. Now kick back for a little deep breathing. Close your eyes and take three long, deep breaths and slowly exhale. You feel better, don't you? Now repeat this whenever the teakettle that is your brain begins to whistle.

Heart Matters
—FINDING PEACE—

Then, because you belong to
Christ Jesus, God will bless you with
peace that no one can completely understand.
And this peace will control the way you think and feel.

PHILIPPIANS 4:7 CEV

My friend Marianne is going blind. A legitimate source of stress and even despair, wouldn't you agree?

Yet Marianne's attitude is anything but frantic. In her calm, steady voice, she explains, "When I start to worry or obsess, I recite the facts I know to be true":

"God is in control."
"He loves me."
"He wants what's best for me, even though my ideas may not be His."
"I will only find peace by resting in His will. Fighting, kicking, and screaming will only lead to a miserable, wasted life."

Because of her failing vision, Marianne, a business manager and gifted crafter, lost her job and the ability to do many of the things she loved. By most standards, she has every right to be angry. Resentful. Bitter. But amazingly, she's not.

"When I could see, I was a control person. I did what I wanted, when I wanted. My prayers consisted mostly of 'Lord, please bless these plans that I've made.' But God didn't say, 'Follow Me when things are great and you have all your faculties.' He said, 'Follow Me even when you're at your worst.' That's when we learn to truly depend on Him for our every need."

Marianne pauses to smile, her liquid brown eyes shining. "I'm not bitter—I'm better. God allowed my blindness in order to grow me. Sure, I get frustrated sometimes and wish I could see, but I wouldn't trade eyesight for this precious peace I have."

Peace, in the midst of life's chaos. Peace, that jumping-off platform for inexplicable joy. Peace, that elusive, anxiety-free place of freedom we long for.

I've been thinking a lot about peace lately. Why is it so hard to grasp? And when we finally do, why does it slip-slide away so quickly?

I've learned that real, honest-to-goodness peace is entirely dependent on our trust in God's sovereignty. That means believing He's in control of all the details of our lives, even if it doesn't *feel* like it. We'll talk a little more about God's sovereignty in chapter 35, but we must realize that only when our trust is anchored in Him can we find peace. There's nothing random or accidental about it. Trust is a decision we make. A volitional, intentional act.

Yes, trust is the cornerstone to acquiring peace. We can relax in complete security, knowing our Creator is looking out for our best interests. Relax. Uncoil. Chill. Let go of the steering wheel.

But when we slide back into the dark, slimy mud hole of thinking *we* are responsible for making things happen in our lives, anxiety and fear take over. The pressure to do it all ourselves eventually shatters any faux pretenses or facade of peace we've erected to prevent the world from seeing our true desperation.

The Old Testament book of Ruth is a wonderful example of God's sovereignty in the life of a gal like you and me. A sister immersed in heartache, loneliness, and financial problems. Yet she found peace amid the turmoil.

Take ten minutes to read Ruth 2 (or better yet, the whole book—it's very short), and notice how all the *random* things that "just happened" to occur weren't really random at all. They were all part of God's sovereign design for Ruth to hook up with Boaz. What a love story! Their Cinderella marriage became strategic in the lineage of King David and then later Jesus Christ Himself.

☙ Ruth, a lonely young widow, went out to find work wheat-gleaning and unknowingly ended up in the field of Boaz, a single, wealthy local celebrity.

☙ Boaz, who was often away traveling, "just happened" to come home when

Ruth was toiling away in his field.

- Although there were likely dozens of women gathering sheaves of grain behind the scores of harvesters, Boaz noticed Ruth.
- Ruth was unafraid to speak her mind but remained very polite and gracious in doing so. What a first impression! Boaz went out of his way to meet her—a dirty, sweaty servant girl out grubbing in the muddy field—something rich landowners just didn't do. This would be like Donald Trump hoofing six flights of stairs to chat with the lady cleaning toilets in one of his buildings.
- In a bold, scandalous move, Boaz invited Ruth to eat with (gasp!) *the men* and even served her lunch himself (*not* a regular occurrence in those days; the women always prepared and served the food then sat apart from the men while they ate). The equivalent today would be Leonardo DiCaprio picking you out of the crowd at a New York movie debut, inviting you to the celebrity party at his home afterward, and then personally whipping up an omelet for you. (Oh baby, don't we wish!)
- Then Boaz asked his servants to discreetly leave extra grain behind in the field for Ruth to make her life easier. I suspect he did this on the sly to preserve Ruth's dignity and so the other girls wouldn't resent her. (Hey, the man was sensitive, too—what a keeper!)

If you read the rest of the story, you'll see that God worked out all the details of Ruth's second-chance romance perfectly. Peace and security were restored to her life after a turbulent season.

We go through turbulent seasons, too, you and I, but we have to remember that the storms won't last forever. Dawn always breaks after a long, dark night. "Weeping may stay for the night, but rejoicing comes in the morning" (Psalm 30:5 NIV).

I find it seriously comforting to know God is just as sovereign today as He was in Ruth's day. He's in control of each and every detail of our lives. And the peace of God, which surpasses all human understanding, *will* keep our hearts and our minds out of the anxiety stress-pool.

Peace is not merely a distant goal that we seek,
but a means by which we arrive at that goal.

MARTIN LUTHER KING JR.

LET'S DECOM-STRESS

1. How do you find peace in the midst of trying circumstances?

2. Let Romans 15:13 percolate in your mind: "May the God of hope fill you with all joy and peace as you trust in him, so that you may overflow with hope by the power of the Holy Spirit" (NIV). What is our first step to becoming filled with joy and peace? What is the result of this infilling? Is this something you desire for yourself?

3. Now reread Philippians 4:7 at the beginning of this chapter. Does God's mysterious peace influence the way you think and feel? Stop right now and ask your heavenly Father to bless you with His unfathomable peace.

Section 4:
Focus on Faith

MARINATING IN FAITH PRODUCES THE
CHOICEST PRIORITY CUTS

Infinite possibilities. . .are born of faith.
MOTHER TERESA

Darth Wader

—Resisting Temptation—

Be on your guard and stay awake.
Your enemy, the devil, is like a roaring lion,
sneaking around to find someone to attack.

1 Peter 5:8 cev

The moon winked from behind a dense canopy of clouds as I ambled the six blocks to my daughter's house after dinner. A warm summer breeze jostled oak branches overhead, creating eerie dancing shadows in pools of light beneath the streetlamps dotting our neighborhood. The sounds of croaking frogs and chirping cicadas drifted from the pond behind the row of houses I was passing.

I was totally lost in thought when suddenly, from behind a shadowy mailbox post, something dark and ominous shot toward me with a horrendous roar. Well, maybe it was more of a squawk, but it seemed very lion-esque at the time.

Anyway, this. . .this *thing* rushed at me from the pitch black night, indefinable and utterly terrifying, its gaping snout aimed strategically at my tender, bare calves. *Snap. Snap.* I couldn't quite make out a shape in the dark.

Ouch! The horrible thing in the night bit me! And it kept on coming, lunging at my heels as I high-stepped down the street, my heart catapulting as my shrieks shredded the peaceful evening ambiance. The frightening creature was surprisingly fast and extremely persistent. I guess I've seen *American Werewolf in London* a few too many times because I just knew I'd sprout chest hair and fangs at the next full moon.

The dreadful beast finally gave up the chase halfway down the block, to the immense entertainment of a man dragging his garbage can to the curb. I could hear him laughing three houses away. I was not amused.

"Met the Phantom Attack Duck, did you?" he called out cheerfully.

"Duck? That nasty creature was a duck? I thought it was a mutant werewolf or a pygmy bear [do they make those?]. . .or at least a tall alligator!" We live in Florida so we have way too many of those. Gators, I mean. Well, maybe not feathered gators.

I bent at the waist to catch my breath and calm my thudding heart.

"Might as well be," the man practically hooted. "Got jaws as strong as a gator. Hurts like a saw blade when she nips ya."

"She?"

"Yup. She's got a nest in those bushes behind the mailbox. Protecting her young. No more vicious creature on this earth than a mad mama. Come after ya like a rabid bulldog, she will. The mailman won't even stop there anymore."

That was my first encounter with the devil in feathers. I call her Darth Wader. At first glance, in broad daylight, from a distance, Darth Wader appears appealingly docile. She resembles Babe's gentle friend Ferdinand. . .only in Goth. But hiker, beware! Appearances can be deceiving.

Instead of a biblical lion, my neighborhood is terrorized by this fierce warrior who strikes fear in the bravest of chests. Our suburban guerrilla is cleverly disguised as long-necked poultry, black as coal from beak to webbed feet. She stands just shy of three feet high but is every bit as imposing as Star Wars' heavy-breathing, black-armored, evil warlord.

"Oh, look," you might naively say, "what an adorable duckie. See how cute she waddles!"

But at night, when a thick blanket of darkness conceals her ebony presence, you'd better watch out! Just like the devil, Darth Wader is sneaking around, ready to attack! I'd heard rumors of her dastardly deeds, tales of innocent, unsuspecting pedestrians tearing through the streets, screaming like homicidal maniacs, but I didn't really believe them. Until it happened to me.

You know, that's how Satan operates, too—hiding out in the peripheral darkness of our lives, blending in and nondescript. Indiscernible. Incognito. Then when we're wandering through our days on autopilot, unaware of his presence and completely off guard, he attacks.

And like Darth Wader, he won't stop dogging us once he's had his first nip,

his first taste of victory.

"I got away with that little fib; one more won't hurt."

"My boss never missed those office supplies I took home; a few more won't matter."

"It's okay to dis my clueless husband in front of my Bible study girlfriends; they won't tell. He'll never know I said anything bad about him."

"I have a prayer request about Liz. You won't believe what she did this time!"

"So the account's overdrawn again; am I supposed to slouch around in rags?"

"Occasionally sneaking in a sexy movie—or novel—is perfectly normal. It's just a little harmless romance. Everybody does it."

But caving to the dark side doesn't *have* to be our destiny, Luke! We have the Force above all other forces, the one true, living God, willing and able to provide armor (for defense) and ammo (for offense) in our ongoing battle against temptation.

Take a gander (pardon the pun!) at the intuitive warning of Ephesians 6:11–17:

> Take everything the Master has set out for you, well-made weapons of the best materials. And put them to use so you will be able to stand up to everything the Devil throws your way. This is no afternoon athletic contest that we'll walk away from and forget about in a couple of hours. This is for keeps, a life-or-death fight to the finish against the Devil and all his angels.
>
> Be prepared. You're up against far more than you can handle on your own. Take all the help you can get, every weapon God has issued, so that when it's all over but the shouting you'll still be on your feet. Truth, righteousness, peace, faith, and salvation are more than words. Learn how to apply them. You'll need them throughout your life. (MSG)

My take on this passage is that whether the breastplate of righteousness is like a chainmail bra guarding our fragile hearts or an iron chemise of faith shielding our soft, exposed underbellies or the helmet-hair of salvation deflecting evil-thought arrows from piercing our minds, God has equipped us to defend ourselves. We just have to make sure our defenses are in place at all times!

The enemy attacks when we're most vulnerable: times of fatigue, illness, or disappointment. He ravages our emotions through heartbreak, resentment, and hatred. He sours our relationships and rips our guts out to weaken us (think *Braveheart* here). He even exploits our secret thoughts, milking them to churn up gossip, slander, criticism.

We don't have to just duck his onslaught! We're mighty warriors! We can fight back with the only undefeatable weapon in existence—the Word of God, sharper than any two-edged sword (see Hebrews 4:12). We must keep our arsenals full of ammo by memorizing verses and studying our Bibles so our flaming arrows are lit and ready to shoot the moment we're jumped by the enemy.

And if, for whatever reason, we can't remove the temptation, we must remove *ourselves* from the temptation. Get thee out of there, girl! Don't stand nekked in front of a speeding freight train! (Nekked is a whole lot different than naked; God created us naked with dignity and beauty, but we make ourselves nekked through disrespect.)

Avoid the devil like I avoid that devilish duck: Take a different route around the pond. Or walk hand in hand with a strong, supportive friend for the same reason I take my yippy little dog along. When it comes to avoiding temptation, two united resisters are infinitely better than one. Especially if one is a barker.

Remember, "Resist the devil and he will flee from you" (James 4:7 NASB). Don't be a wimp! Be a warrior! Why settle for Olive Oyl when you could be Xena?

Satan, like Darth Wader, is lurking for helpless victims. Girlfriend, let's refuse to be sitting ducks!

Opportunity knocks softly,
but temptation parks its fat derriere
on the doorbell, scarfing chocolate.

DEBORA M. COTY

Let's Decom-stress

1. Who or what is the Darth Wader in your life? When are you most vulnerable to temptation?

2. How do you best access the Force (God's power) when battle is imminent?

3. How about preparing your artillery and lighting a flaming arrow right now by memorizing James 4:7? (It's short but powerful— I guarantee it will come in handy next time your Darth Wader tries to take a plug out of your tender flesh!)

Luther's Legacy
—UNCONDITIONAL LOVE—

Love never gives up,
never loses faith, is always hopeful,
and endures through every circumstance.

1 CORINTHIANS 13:7 NLT

I screamed as a dark, flailing body swung through the air and landed on my little-girl shoulders. A thick, furry tail immediately coiled around my neck, and bony, agile fingers began picking through my hair. Sharp, white teeth flashed by my face as an odd, musky odor slapped me in the face. A long chain dangled from the tree limb above my head, attached to a cat collar around the waist of the wiry creature now poking an inquisitive finger into my ear.

"Don't panic," my school chum Dianne said. She had forgotten to warn me about her family's unusual pet living in the tall tree beside their home. "Luther won't bite if you stay calm. He just wants to see what you're made of."

Luther*, a brown-capped capuchin ringtail monkey, was truly a soul in need of grace. He constantly got into unimaginable trouble just by being himself. The black "monk's cap" on his furry head disguised the propensity for peril constantly percolating in his tiny maniacal brain.

Shortly after his arrival at Dianne's house, Luther's cage was brought inside one frigid winter night. Instead of being appreciative, his nimble fingers had no difficulty unfastening the cage door's wire latch from whence he leaped onto the kitchen counter, dumped out canisters of flour and sugar, and mixed them together with his dexterous little hands.

When he got bored with his redecorating project, the mischievous monkey discovered the box of tissues on the counter and pulled them out one by one, throwing them into the air like tiny parachutes.

Luther was soon delegated to the tree in the backyard, where he could explore to his heart's delight, using his strong tail curled into a ring (thus his species name) to climb, swing along branches, and usher cats up for a surprise visit. He loved to swoop down and snatch unsuspecting felines passing by, carry them up to his A-frame tree house, and lay them gently on his little front porch for a flea-picking good time. When the grooming sessions ended, he'd let his victims loose to scamper back down while he busily unscrewed porch lightbulbs to smash on the ground or ransacked trash cans for ketchup bottles or Coke cans to upend for a tasty treat.

At night, Luther fashioned a blanket for himself with any kind of rag or doormat he could find. He'd throw it over his head and pull it around his thin body so only his little face peeked out, then settle down to sleep in a comfortable squat.

He was like a baby in many ways. He loved to be snuggled and crooned to in a soft voice by his humans. He responded with tiny *huh, huh* sounds that indicated he was happy and loved them back, much like a cat purring.

But he just couldn't leave well enough alone, even if it was to his own detriment. Luther pulled and tugged at his water bucket, which had been nailed to the tree, until he dumped it over, leaving him awfully thirsty. A heavy metal washtub worked for a while, until Luther began baptizing kittens.

He twisted off water faucet handles to make them gush like fire hydrants. A dripping water hose became his lifeline, although it left his monkey-run beneath the tree perpetually muddy. His favorite pastime was slapping his hand over the nozzle to spray unsuspecting visitors.

So why would anyone put up with such a troublemaker, you might ask. Who needs the angst? Wouldn't it be easier to buy a nice calm goldfish?

The answer is simple but profound: because Dianne's family loved the little fellow. Despite his flaws, which were legion. Regardless of the messes he managed to get himself into. No matter how many times they had to clean him up, rush to his rescue, or protect him from himself. They loved him unconditionally—a love not based on behavior or merit or whether he deserved it or not.

Just like the way Papa God loves us.

"Long before he laid down earth's foundations, he had us in mind, had settled

on us as the focus of his love, to be made whole and holy by his love" (Ephesians 1:4 MSG). Did you catch that? God's love for us isn't dependent on anything we do or don't do, blab or omit. Our Father's love itself is what makes us whole and holy; not anything we can contrive, create, or earn. And He's had us—you and me—in mind to be the focus of His love even before the creation of our world.

What a calming, reassuring thought. Such indescribable security. To know that we are truly loved, *regardless.* No matter how many times we blow it. In the midst of our own self-inflicted messes; when the hairy burdens of our day weigh heavily on our shoulders and wrap their choking tails around our necks. We are unconditionally loved when creatures of darkness attach themselves to us and threaten to sink sharp teeth into our vulnerable flesh, just to see what we're made of.

Even if we react poorly, even if stress transforms us into unrecognizable, destructive creatures, there's a way out. If we only remember Luther's legacy.

We are treasured. Cherished. Adored. Papa God wants nothing more than to cuddle with us, crooning His comfort and peace into our troubled hearts. Anytime. Anywhere. He never gives up on us, never loses hope in us, and endures through every circumstance.

And, sister, He doesn't monkey around.

*Luther's hilarious exploits were lovingly documented by his human mom, Lila Rae Caldwell Yawn.

Love has nothing to do with what you are expecting to get—only with what you are expecting to give—which is everything.

KATHARINE HEPBURN

LET'S DECOM-STRESS

1. I, like Luther, tend to persist in my stubbornness to my own detriment, not realizing my folly until it's too late. I've tipped over far too many water buckets and then complained of thirst. In which ways do you identify with Luther?

2. How do 1 Corinthians 13:7 and Ephesians 1:4 relate to those of us who are so much like obstinate, naughty Luther?

3. In what specific ways does Papa God's unconditional love make you feel cuddled, cherished, peaceful?

Dead Last
—COURAGE—

*For God has not given us a spirit of fear and timidity,
but of power, love, and self-discipline.*
2 TIMOTHY 1:7 NLT

I am so lost, I lamented. *How can I get this mixed up in a city I've lived in for thirty years?*

I had just seen a landmark that made me realize I was miles in the opposite direction of my destination. I steered off the busy street onto a nearly deserted side road to turn around. *For heaven's sake, Lord, why did You make me so directionally challenged? Ella's concert will be over by the time I get there.*

At that moment, something unusual caught my eye in the roadway ahead. Reducing my speed, I did a double take. Could it really be a body? I gasped in disbelief. A man. . .an elderly Indian man in a white tunic was lying supine on the asphalt. An empty car was parked nearby, its engine running and passenger door standing wide open.

Could it be a trick? I'd heard of criminals using such a ploy to dupe unsuspecting good Samaritans. Confusion whirled in my brain.

I was late for my girlfriend's big singing debut and plenty annoyed. For some inexplicable reason, after I'd punched in the address, my GPS sent me to a vacant lot on the wrong side of town instead of to the concert venue. What had gotten into that stupid machine?

Now there was a body in the road. Good grief. Surely someone else would stop. My practical inner voice recited all the reasons why it couldn't possibly be me:

I'm too dressed up—I have on my glittery black hat, for pity's sake.
There might be blood. Germs. AIDS.

My friends are expecting me; they'll worry if I don't show up.
What can I do anyway if this poor guy's legitimately in trouble?

But then my selfish thoughts were superimposed by a scripture I'd heard a thousand times: "Whatever you did for one of the least of these brothers and sisters of mine, you did for me" (Matthew 25:40 NIV). That verse always seemed so neat and clean in the pages of my Bible. But in real life, I had a feeling it could get pretty messy.

Okay, Papa God, I get it. You want me to stop. I hope it's true that You send special protection for children and fools. We both know which I am.

I jerked to a stop, grabbed my keys, locked the car, and tottered over in my black Italian heels to the unmoving man. His dark eyes, glazed and unseeing, stared skyward from a steel-gray face. A young man in his thirties moved into view from the other side of the car, gesturing wildly as he spoke in heavily accented English into a cell phone. "My father. . .heart disease. . .diabetes, too. . .no, *no*—I cannot. . .I don't know how to do CPR!"

His desperate eyes caught mine and a glimmer of hope flickered there. The unspoken question hung suspended in the sizzling late-afternoon June heat. Could I—*would* I—help?

I lambasted Papa God in my head. *Me? Oh no, not me, Lord! What are You thinking? You know I'm not good in emergencies. I'll either throw up or faint.* And then I glanced at the helpless man lying at my feet, his life slowly ebbing away. What if it were my own father?

Gulping down the wad of fear in my throat, I nodded to the guy on the phone and hiked up my long black skirt to kneel beside the fallen man. *Please help me remember how to do this!* I shot heavenward.

My cardiopulmonary resuscitation wasn't just rusty; it was downright decrepit. It had been years since I took a lifesaving course, and I simply could *not* get the hang of resuscitating that dummy. I was dead last in my class. I remembered all too well the instructor's thinly veiled irritation as he signed my card just to get rid of me after everyone else had already gone home.

The son gave panicked directions to the 911 operator while my clammy fingers searched for a carotid pulse in the older man's neck. Nothing. No breath, either. For the life of me, I could *not* recall the ratio of chest compressions to mouth-to-mouth breaths.* Was it 8:2 or 20:5? I just couldn't remember. Why hadn't I paid more attention in class?

My thoughts were jumbled. *Lord, I'm scared out of my wits here. What if this ends in disaster because of my mistakes? Please send someone who knows what they're doing.* I frantically scanned the tree-lined street. Empty. *Oh no. I'm just not qualified. I'm not able. I'm afraid.* Is this how Moses felt when God sent him—a runaway, stuttering shepherd—to be the rescuer of a nation?

A scripture filled my head. "I can do all things through Him [Christ] who strengthens me" (Philippians 4:13 NASB).

Even me?

Even you, daughter.

Take a deep breath. Exhale. I settle on a 10:3 ratio, figuring something was better than nothing.

"I can do all things through Christ who strengthens me." Eyes close momentarily. Get a grip. Okay, Debbie. Just do it!

I began pumping away at the man's chest, interspersing puffs of air into his upturned mouth as I pinched his nose closed. Astounding thoughts besieged me as I labored: *I should ditch my hat—the brim keeps bumping his face; no, I have terrible hat-hair; leave it on. Aren't these tunics gorgeous? Such exquisite fabric. It's getting filthy on the ground; what a shame—his wife probably spent hours ironing it. Isn't it weird how the prints from my Berry Surprise lipstick crisscross his mouth like that? Wait a minute. What am I thinking? Shouldn't I be more spiritual at a time like this?*

After the third CPR cycle, the victim's chin quivered and he moaned faintly. Two other drivers (both men) had gathered by this time and helped roll him onto his side as he vomited. I could hear the EMS siren in the distance, and although he was still unconscious, I felt a surge of hope for this stranger I suddenly cared about so deeply.

"We need to keep it going." The words came out of my mouth even as I cringed at the residue of vomit on the blue-tinted lips before me. I gazed at the other two bystanders, hoping at least one would offer relief. No takers. My stomach lurched at the thought of more mouth-to-mouth. But a man's life was at stake here. Thankfully, it wasn't necessary. Before I'd finished another round of compressions, the ambulance was there; EMTs swarmed the scene.

I stood with the distraught son as the beautiful tunic was cut from his father's barely breathing body and was loaded into the ambulance, his face covered with an oxygen mask. I felt a heart-bond with these family members, although I never learned their names. We were so very different on the surface, yet so much alike beneath. I offered another silent prayer for them as I watched the ambulance drive away.

Returning to my car, I was trembling so violently that I couldn't turn the ignition key. I somehow managed to dig my cell phone from my purse to call Chuck but it skittered across the floorboard. Tears finally came. I felt like a gushing fire hydrant.

It occurred to me that I shouldn't have even been there. If the GPS hadn't sent me right instead of left, I'd have been on the far side of town, drinking chai lattes and obliviously enjoying a concert. . .as a man lay dying. And if I hadn't randomly decided to turn around on that particular street, crucial minutes would have been lost.

But, of course, our God is not a random God. How perfectly obvious that He had orchestrated all the details, even to the use of an underqualified, overdressed rescuer who was dead last in her resuscitation class. For His specialty, His forte, His marvelous operational technique is to use inadequate, frightened people to serve as His hands and feet. Yahweh's courage is more than enough.

It's brilliant, really. Then there's no doubt whom the *real* rescuer is.

The American Heart Association currently recommends only continuous chest compressions (omitting mouth-to-mouth breathing) at a rate of 100 per minute.

You gain strength, courage, and confidence by every experience in which you really stop to look fear in the face. You must do the thing which you think you cannot do.

ELEANOR ROOSEVELT

LET'S DECOM-STRESS

1. When was a time you depended on God's courage when yours was inadequate?

2. Can you think of circumstances when God used divine intervention—like my malfunctioning GPS—to put you in the right place at the right time to accomplish something as His hands and feet? Be assured that He has; sometimes we have to open up the hood to see the engine making the car run.

3. Spend a little time meditating on the amazing possibilities presented by Philippians 4:13: "I can do all things through Him who strengthens me" (NASB). Commit this one to memory, sister. Learn it. Love it. Live it.

Kneels on Wheels
—PRAYER—

*"Call on me and come and pray
to me, and I will listen to you."*
JEREMIAH 29:12 NIV

Okay, I'll admit it's nontraditional, wacky, maybe even a smidge juvenile. But hey, it works for me! I'm referring to my mountaintop prayer partner, Sir Lancelot. Instead of flesh and blood, he runs on oil and gasoline. Lance is a four-wheeler.

Sir Lancelot's predecessor, Trigger, was my first ATV. I acquired him on a whim as I drove home from work on my fortieth birthday, feeling mighty old. Trigger, no youngster himself and sporting a FOR SALE sign because of it, beckoned to me from a stranger's front yard. His cold metallic carburetor and my warm-blooded heart immediately bonded.

Spouse insisted on relocating Trigger (spouting something silly about finding a place where I could cause the least amount of damage) to our cabin in the remote Smoky Mountains. Trigger and I spent many a glorious vacation together exploring mountainous terrain. Alas, poor Trigger finally chugged his last exhaust (I've no doubt lawn mower and motorcycle heaven admitted him by excellent referral from St. Peter himself), and Sir Lancelot soon came to live at our cabin.

Sir Lancelot's noble name was bequeathed because of his un-noble propensity toward flatu-*lance. . .a lot.* Although a robust climber, Lance tends to toot/ pass gas/backfire going downhill. (My apologies to the reader with delicate sensibilities.) When this occurs, my heart seizes and I often duck, thinking revengeful, rifle-toting bears are taking pot shots at me from behind trees.

I consider my trail time straddling Sir Lancelot my most effective and ardent prayer time. Especially in the fall of the year, when God's paintbrush has been

busy and leaves as colorful as Joseph's famed coat line mountain trails and crunch beneath the hooves of my trusty twenty-first-century steed.

Now, I've never ridden many horses, but riding Sir Lancelot is as close a simulation as I'm going to get. My previous equine experience consists of a stout pony at the end of a county fair rope when I was five years old, and at thirty-two, bronco busting a terrorist roan reluctant to continue her trek through Colorado snow two feet deep. Having had her apparent fill of our frigid trail hike, she suddenly reared up on her hind legs (yep, just like the Lone Ranger's Silver. . .only a little screamier), swiveled 180 degrees, and made a mad dash for the warm barn with me hanging on for dear life. I was nearly decapitated when forced into a backbend in the saddle to avoid a low beam.

Faithful Lance has never run away, although there were a few times I flew one direction and he another when traversing a tricky patch of rocky creek bed. He never complains, throws a shoe, or requires a vet. All he asks for is a pail of petrol and a warm blanket on chilly nights (a tarp will do).

And oh, the rich prayer life I experience four-wheeling through the wooded hills—meeting my Lord face-to-face in His mountaintop cathedral. It's not at all words that evoke worship, but simply basking in God's presence. A precious opportunity to be quiet and listen for His still, small voice whispering to my soul. Mother Teresa, prayer warrior tiny in stature but enormous in spirit, once said, "God speaks in the silence of the heart. Listening is the beginning of prayer."

The crisp air whistles through my hair, the sun warms my back, flying bugs settle between my teeth, and I praise God for the magnificence of His creation. I come *alive*, realizing with due remorse that the balance of my time is spent in a mostly dead state.

I don't want to approach prayer as a chore. I'm not reporting for duty or giving God instructions on what's best for me. Nor do I want my prayer life to consist merely of rhino-in-the-road desperation pleas to NeedGodNOW.com.

Above all, I don't want to get caught up in religion and miss the relationship. To get so busy learning about Him and doing a gazillion things that I call serving Him that I neglect to get to *know* Him. That's when Christianity becomes "nice-ianity" and all about behavior—rights and wrongs—rather than about a dynamic, daily communication with a living, loving Savior.

No, I come with a humble heart, an open mind, and a thirsty spirit. I *cherish* spending time with Him. No one says we have to kneel or fold our hands or bow our heads to pray. "Certain thoughts are prayers. There are moments when, whatever be the attitude of the body, the soul is on its knees" (Victor Hugo, *Les Misérables*).

The striking contrast of gold, crimson, and burnt orange leaves against a cobalt blue sky draws me into His throne room, where I feel God's presence through every vibrant inch of me. His warming love surrounds me, encompasses me, soaks me through and through.

On second thought, that soaking part is probably because I forgot to pick up my feet when I forged the crick. (Up here they're not creeks; they're cricks.)

Nevertheless, Sir Lancelot helps me fulfill the biblical mandate to "pray without ceasing" (1 Thessalonians 5:17 NASB). Prayer, being less of an event and more of a mind-set, is ever so much more an integral part, no, the *whole* of my existence when I'm communing with my Creator on a moment-by-moment, day-by-day basis.

We all need a prayer partner to help transport us to God's throne room. So tell me, who, or *what*, is your Sir Lancelot?

It is not well for a man to pray
cream and live skim milk.

HENRY WARD BEECHER

LET'S DECOM-STRESS

1. Is prayer more of a single event or a continuous mind-set for you? Prayer can become our last resort rather than our first resort if we don't regard communication with Christ as important as breathing. Even before our prayers are answered, we benefit from the immense blessing of His loving company.

2. Spending time in God's presence is where it all begins. . . acceptance, peace, transformation. Even though we may keep prayer lines open on a minute-by-minute basis during our busy day, we need occasional extended periods of uninterrupted soak time. Go to your calendar right now and schedule some quality time with your Papa God for the upcoming week. He wants to spend time with you!

3. Do you have a prayer partner—flesh, metallic, or otherwise? How about nailing one down today?

Everyday Miracles
—God's Sovereignty—

We can make our plans,
but the Lord determines our steps.

Proverbs 16:9 NLT

I took a bite of breakfast cereal as I rubbed my sleepy eyes and turned the pages of the *Tampa Tribune* one early January morning. Whoa, doggies! I almost spewed my Wheaties as my own life-sized face smiled back. Well, it wasn't quite life-sized, but it was sure big enough to highlight the crow's feet and under-eye carry-on. Wouldn't you think newspapers might have magical picture putty to doctor that?

Anyway, I was shocked at the full-page article in the main section. (I knew a piece was coming but thought it would be much smaller and tucked into a back page somewhere.) I felt completely overwhelmed by this unmerited blessing, that Papa God had arranged the details of my life to start out the new year with such lovely affirmation of His hand on my life. His fingerprints were all over that wonderful surprise! I rejoiced in the assurance that He was constantly at work, ironing out plans to use my meager gifts and abilities in His service and for His good pleasure (see Philippians 2:13).

He's the Lord of details, you know. And He loves to surprise us.

One of my favorite biblical stories proving this has always been when Jesus' disciples were sent to search for a place to have the Passover dinner (Last Supper) and found that Jesus had prearranged all the details down to the man meeting them with a pitcher of water on his head (see Mark 14:12–16).

This was most unusual, for men didn't tote water in that day—it was considered women's work. Out of the male realm. It would be like Jack Nicholson being named the new CoverGirl spokesperson.

It came to my attention last Christmas season that the same divine attention to detail was true of events surrounding Jesus' birth: Mary's miraculous manless pregnancy, the census being taken at the exact time to place Mary and Joseph in Bethlehem (many miles from their home in Nazareth) for Jesus' birth to fulfill the prophecy of Micah 5:2, and the presence of an extraordinarily bright star (see Matthew 2:2) to announce the long-awaited Messiah's arrival.

Some believe that the guiding star was actually two planets, Venus and Jupiter, lining up in the heavens on this sublime occasion to appear as one doubly bright heavenly night-light. Regardless of whether God played supernatural chess with the planets or created a separate spotlight just for the occasion, He must've begun the process decades before.

And consider the wise men who followed the star to find baby Jesus (see Matthew 2:1–21). God had prearranged all the details w-a-y in advance. Daniel had been captured and taken to Babylon five hundred years before. The magi, descendants of Daniel's people and remnants of his Jewish faith in a decidedly non-Jewish land, traveled nine hundred miles for more than a year to arrive at just the right time to offer their costly gifts to Mary and Joseph on Jesus' behalf. The gold, frankincense, and myrrh they brought funded the dirt-poor holy family's emergency flight to Egypt (just after the magi's last camel disappeared over the hill) to save Jesus from the death raid of jealous King Herod.

No coincidences, these. Just like there are no coincidences in the *grace notes* of our lives. Grace notes—the little daily special touches from Papa God that let us know He's got our backs—are the everyday miracles that reflect God's sovereignty, His supreme power and authority over every detail of our lives.

One of my favorite personal grace notes involves a gal I met a few years ago. During our first conversation, I sensed that Gina was searching for something to fill the God-shaped hole in her life, and the Holy Spirit had been preparing her heart for His presence. Gina had previously had a bad experience with "judgmental church people" and was hesitant to subject herself to painful rejection again. I wanted to prove to her that real Christ-followers don't shoot the wounded, but instead are happy to lead them by the hand to healing through Christ.

On the spur of the moment, I invited Gina to come to church and sit with

my family. The implications hit me only afterward. The problem was that Gina was a smoker and I'm highly allergic to smoke. Every time I'm anywhere near it, my eyes, ears, throat, and nasal passages itch like crazy and start constricting. I end up clawing my face and choking like a cat with a furball.

The first Sunday Gina came to church, she was late. I suspected she'd been delayed by the tug-of-war within herself as to whether to risk coming or not. The service had already begun when she arrived, and she, looking totally embarrassed, had to climb over four laps to reach the empty chair beside me. Both my husband and daughter, well aware of my allergy, cast covert disparaging glances my way as she passed, for Gina had apparently indulged in a cigarette or two on the way to church. Smoke fumes saturated her clothes and hair like supersonic death rays. I was Clark Kent and she was kryptonite.

I lobbed a "Please help me, Lord!" prayer, gave Gina a hug of welcome, and steeled myself for the Debbie meltdown show to begin.

But nothing happened. Not one scratch or hack or cough. And better yet, the Master of Everyday Miracles blocked my smoke allergy not only that day, but every single Sunday for the two years Gina sat by me in church. Oh, I still lapsed into my regular allergic reactions when around smokers in restaurants or amusement parks or ball games, but never once in church beside Gina as God's redeeming love poured over us both.

Doesn't it knock boulders of stress from our weary, sagging shoulders to realize that God's sovereignty, His ultimate authority over this universe He created, takes precedence over the tiny pebbles of control we thought we had? Striving and struggling and toiling to control the course of our lives doesn't depend on *us*, sister, for He's the CEO, the Big Guy in Charge, the Buck Stops Here desk. "Nothing in all creation is hidden from God's sight" (Hebrews 4:13 NIV).

It's humbling and incredibly encouraging to know the Creator of the universe somehow finds the time to manage even the smallest details of our lives. It makes it much easier to trust Him with the big stuff, doesn't it?

Coincidence is God's way
of staying anonymous.
ALBERT EINSTEIN

LET'S DECOM-STRESS

1. Okay, think of a time the Master of Everyday Miracles prearranged all the details of a particular event in your life. Now think of another. Do you see a pattern?

2. How do these grace notes affirm that God's hand is on your life? Can you discern His fingerprints?

3. Take a moment to praise our Lord and Savior for His all-powerful sovereignty. Remember, He's large and in charge!

Lost and Found
—FAITH—

*"If you had faith even as small as a
mustard seed, you could say to this mountain,
'Move from here to there,' and it would move.
Nothing would be impossible."*
MATTHEW 17:20 NLT

I pull into my garage and pop open the trunk. My arms, already overflowing with bags from the front seat, threaten to give way as I combine as many items as possible with the groceries in back and haul them inside, trip after trip.

After slamming the trunk, I reach through the front passenger window for my purse, which lives on the little table thingie between the seats. It's not there.

This is not terribly alarming because my Big Bertha pocketbook has been known to, under the gravitational effects of inertia, launch from its little vehicular home like a guided missile when my brakes are forcefully engaged. Which is often.

Nope, it's not on the floorboards either.

Well, sometimes said purse plays roller derby, depending upon which direction my car was turning when the inertia took effect. So with much grunting and groaning, I grope beneath the seats and then along their sides. I unearth three pens; two fossilized apple cores; a stiff, blackened banana peel (so *that's* why I have a craving for banana bread every time I drive!); a dog-eared bookmark; $1.37 in change; the grocery list I lost three months ago; a package of dried-out hand wipes; a crusty fork; an almost-empty yogurt cup; and a tube of mascara. But no purse. I scan the underbellies of the backseats (my reverse driving has occasionally been compared to a bat flying out of somewhere exceptionally hot), but no sign of my purse.

Okay, now I'm starting to freak.

Lost my pocketbook? Oh no, no, no! I can't lose that—*everything* is in there! My driver's license, credit cards, checkbook, insurance cards, receipts for all the clothes I need to return, my reading glasses, enough food to live for a month on a desert island, and most importantly, the last cherished square of that amazing German chocolate bar I bought on vacation last year.

It couldn't possibly all be gone! Tell me it ain't so!

I envision myself setting my handbag on top of my car to unlock my door and forgetting it's there and driving off. Gulp. I actually did that once with my CD case. Can you say crunchy vinyl? The innards of my purse could be strung out anywhere in the five miles between the grocery store and home. Haystack. Needles. *No!*

My overactive imagination kicks in and I picture a juvenile delinquent bicycle gang gathering my personal belongings like an Easter egg hunt and purchasing fourteen crates of Laffy Taffy with my credit cards. My angst transitions into rage when the nose-ringed, Goth-haired punk in my mind smirks as he slides the last bite of my German chocolate bar onto his bolted tongue.

With heart racing, I storm into the kitchen to call the police. Forgetting the grocery bags lined up just inside the door, I trip and sprawl belly first on the tile floor, surrounded by scattering grapes, rolling cantaloupes, canned beans, and. . .my goodness, what is that? Lo and behold, it's my upended purse, liberated from the grocery bag I'd apparently stuffed it in when my memory was hibernating.

Whew! What relief! The knots in my stomach begin to uncoil. The banjo strings that were my neck cords relax. My purse was lost and now it's found. I was blind but now I see.

Life is so like that. We search everywhere for answers and get uptight and stressed out when the source of knowledge is in our possession the whole time. It's called the Bible.

During my two-year depression following six heart-wrenching miscarriages, I searched for answers: Why? How could a loving God allow this to happen when we'd prayed and earnestly sought His guidance before each and every pregnancy? Had He abandoned me? It certainly felt like it. Or was He never really there to begin with?

Hard questions. Questions that either shape or shatter our faith. The kind each of us face when we're beaten down by devastating loss. When we can't pray and feel utterly hopeless. Lost without a map.

For a solid year I found no answers. Trite, canned platitudes from well-meaning people did nothing but infuriate me: "It's God's will—just accept it." "Look for the good in every situation." "If you had enough faith, you wouldn't find this so difficult."

Well, apparently I *didn't* have enough faith. Even after living as a Christ-follower for twenty-five years, I wasn't sure I had any faith at all. The hollowness in my soul threatened to devour me whole. Spiritual insecurity added more stress to my already overwhelmed existence.

In unadorned desperation, I turned to my Bible. The only place I *hadn't* looked.

I began reading the psalms, identifying with David as he bared his wounded heart. I found solace in the scream-at-God verses, like: "I dissolve my couch with my tears" (6:6 NASB); "I am poured out like water. . .my heart is like wax. . .melted within me" (22:14 NASB); "My sorrow is continually before me" (38:17 NASB); "Why do You hide Your face and forget our affliction and oppression?" (44:24 NASB); "My heart is in anguish within me" (55:4 NASB); "I looked for sympathy, but there was none, and for comforters, but I found none" (69:20 NASB); "Why do you withdraw Your hand?" (74:11 NASB); "I am so troubled that I cannot speak" (77:4 NASB); "You have taken me up and thrown me aside" (102:10 NIV); "Bring my soul out of prison" (142:7 NASB); and "My spirit is overwhelmed" (143:4 NASB).

David's cries of despair became my prayers—the only communication with God I could muster. But they cracked open the door. Gradually, over many months, the rock that was my heart began to crack from the inside out. God blessed my reluctant obedience in seeking nourishment—no, life itself—from His Word.

Sometimes when we feel least like doing something, it's the very thing we need to do most. I kept reading every day out of sheer obedience and progressed to the help-me-trust-again psalm verses like: "The LORD is my shepherd, I shall not want. . . . Your rod and Your staff, they comfort me" (23:1, 4 NASB); "Turn to me and be gracious to me, for I am lonely and afflicted" (25:16 NASB); "Weeping may last for the night, but a shout of joy comes in the morning" (30:5 NASB); "Be

gracious to me, O LORD, for I am in distress" (31:9 NASB); "I sought the LORD, and He answered me, and delivered me from all my fears" (34:4 NASB); "Rest in the LORD and wait patiently for Him" (37:7 NASB); "Why, my soul, are you downcast? . . . Put your hope in God, for I will yet praise him" (42:11 NIV); and "Cease striving and know that I am God" (46:10 NASB). Other psalms offering hope and healing are 56, 63, 119, 121, and 139.

Within those pages I'd stumbled upon a map, but I didn't realize I was actually clawing my way out of my lost, dark cavern until I saw light peeking over the rim.

God's Word seeped into my parched spirit like a healing spring of water. By praying through the psalms, something unexplainable changed inside me. My circumstances hadn't been altered. I still had no sweet baby to cuddle. But somehow a seed of trust in the Great Healer had taken root and bloomed inside me like a fragrant flower.

I was once again able to praise my heavenly Father through psalms like: "You, LORD, are. . .the One who lifts my head high" (3:3 NIV); "In peace I will both lie down and sleep" (4:8 NASB); "He does not forget the cry of the afflicted" (9:12 NASB); "I love you, O LORD, my strength" (18:1 NASB); "We will sing for joy over your victory" (20:5 NASB); "My flesh and my heart may fail, but God is the strength of my heart and my portion forever" (73:26 NASB); "How blessed is the man who trusts in You!" (84:12 NASB); "He will cover you with his feathers, and under his wings you will find refuge" (91:4 NIV); "Great is the LORD and greatly to be praised" (96:4 NASB); "The LORD is good; His lovingkindness is everlasting and His faithfulness to all generations" (100:5 NASB); "I love the LORD, for he heard my voice; he heard my cry for mercy" (116:1 NIV); and "He heals the brokenhearted and binds up their wounds" (147:3 NIV).

After this searching process—and it is a process, not a sudden discovery—my relationship with my loving heavenly Father was fully and gloriously restored. Supernatural peace soothed my tattered nerves.

Healing takes effort on our part; we can't just sit like a limp, wounded lump and wait for it to hit us. We have to dig deep for the courage to reach out for help from the very source of our pain. Or so we perceive. But then by God's grace we *will* find what was really never lost.

On a lighter note, I believe misplacing things like my purse is hormonal. Of course, I blame everything on hormones. Just haven't figured out why the fewer hormones I have as I age, the more things I lose. I have noticed, though, that the things I've found that once were lost become oh, so much more precious.

Like faith. And German chocolate. Mmm.

Faith can move mountains, but don't be surprised if God hands you a shovel.

UNKNOWN

LET'S DECOM-STRESS

1. Have you ever gone through a time when you felt like you had lost your faith? How did you find it again?

2. When you feel wounded, where do you turn for healing?

3. Remember this chapter, dear sister, and the next time you feel that your pain is estranging you from God, begin praying through the psalms I've outlined. You will not believe how lifting God's Word up to Him in prayer will miraculously mend your broken heart. I'm praying for you.

Feed the Fever
—Worship—

Could that man possibly fit one more thing into my gaping mouth?

I had been at the dentist's office for hours already, and it looked as if I was in for at least two more. The necessary procedure required that I sit still (pure torture for the girl one step beyond ADD) while a sadistic dentist stuffed into my mouth everything in the office that wasn't cemented down.

My weary jaws, cranked wider than a bear trap, bore a three-hundred-pound linebacker's molded plastic mouthpiece (at least that's what it felt like), enough cotton to petticoat both Scarlet O'Hara and Mammy, one of those bent metal mirrors on a stick, a miner's pickax, and a few dozen tongue depressors to stir it all around.

Oh, did I forget to mention a pair of gloved hands the size of baseball mitts?

My chair had been tilted to handstand position and some kind of offensive gray goo with an odor reminiscent of the frogs we dissected in biology class was inserted with great liberality so that my tongue would have something to chase down my gullet. Then Dr. Openwide, in his sternest voice, warned, "Do *not* squirm, Mrs. Coty, or we'll have to do it all over again. I'll be back in fifteen minutes. Do you think you can be still for that long?"

I started to remind him that I was a grown woman, for pity's sake, but the hangy ball at the back of my throat suddenly twisted itself around the pillars of hardware in my mouth. All that would come out was "Ahrrrrrr."

Frowning, Dr. Openwide ripped off his gloves, wagged a warning finger at me, flipped off the overhead lights, and left the room. He was just grumpy because earlier when he'd said, "Close," I did. Hard. How was I to know that sausage he calls a thumb was between my molars?

Oh, man. A fifteen-minute sentence of imprisonment? Arrgh! It might as well be fifteen years for me. At least I had one small diversion: the iPod in my purse that was hanging strategically on the arm of my dental chair. I had anticipated such a time as this. Trying not to turn my head, I contorted myself into an S shape to grope the contents of my purse until I could locate my tiny electronic deliverer. Ah, there it was.

Inserting earbuds, I switched on the iPod and suddenly my head was filled with praise music. Wonderful, uplifting, heart-swelling, bebopping praise music that made me forget all about my pathetic throbbing gums. Boogie-holic that I am, my restrained toetapping soon progressed to foot jiving and then knee knocking.

By the time I hit Carolyn Arends's "I Can Hear You," one of my all-time spirited faves about hearing God's voice in the midst of everyday chaos, I couldn't help but add a little hip action. Before I knew it, my hands were swaying in midair, my bouncing head kept time, and I lapsed into a kind of horizontal rocked-out praise wriggle.

Luke 19:39–40 (see the beginning of this chapter) sprang to life when the inanimate objects around me joined in my little praise fest: the tray of dental tools hopped to the beat, stray cotton balls bounced across the treatment table, even the long-necked Cyclops spotlight staring down at me nodded its hinged head in time.

I was totally transported out of that sterile dental cubicle into the throne room of my King. Whoa! I was doing church!

No need to elaborate upon uptight Dr. Openwide's wigged-out overreaction when he walked past the door, for that is not my point. (Besides, I think it's rude to call someone "Nightmare on Crown Street," don't you?) I try to be patient with him because I figure either the poor man's boxers are too tight or he needs deliverance, bless his teensy little heart.

Okay, so maybe I got a little carried away. But my point is that worship

doesn't have to be just in a stained-glass building or magnificent cathedral or at a designated hour and location. The true church isn't an edifice; it's the people, the worshippers inside. It's us, you and me. "The *real* believers are the ones the Spirit of God leads to work away at this ministry, filling the air with Christ's praise as we do it" (Philippians 3:3 MSG).

Yep, we spontaneous worshippers, the ones who burst forth with unbridled praise springing from a joyful spirit, are just the kind of worshippers the Father is looking for. "Yet a time is coming and has now come when the true worshipers will worship the Father in the Spirit and in truth, for they are the kind of worshipers the Father seeks" (John 4:23 NIV).

So, girlfriend, we can do church anywhere, anytime. Papa God loves it when we do. The Holy Spirit is ready and willing to meet us, greet us, fill us, and fulfill us at the drop of a paper dental bib. . .or in a carpool line. . .or in a McDonald's drive-through. He will be there, smiling. All we have to supply is wonder, awe, and a heart full of praise.

Wonder is involuntary praise.

EDWARD YOUNG

LET'S DECOM-STRESS

1. Have you ever been so moved that you burst forth in spontaneous worship? If not, you should try it sometime. . .there's nothing so exhilarating!

2. You don't have to possess an overly animated personality to "do church" anywhere the Spirit moves you; quiet worship is just as pleasing to God as overt praise. But hey, you'll never know what you're missing if you don't step outside your comfort zone (in privacy, of course) and praise your Creator with every fiber of you He created. Sing,

twirl, lift your hands, shout, laugh, cry, tap dance, jig, whatever. . .
if it's done in a spirit of praise, honor, and gratitude, He'll love it!

3. What leads you most toward worship? Make it a point to subject yourself to that particular thing sometime this week.

Taking the Plunge
—TRUST—

*Trust in the LORD with all
your heart; do not depend
on your own understanding.
Seek his will in all you do, and he
will show you which path to take.*

PROVERBS 3:5–6 NLT

Splash!

My heart pounded as the twelve-year-old schnauzer flailed in panic and his head submerged beneath the churning surface of the water.

I had been doggie-sitting at my sister's house for the past week while she and her family were on vacation. It was late, after 10:00 p.m., and I'd just returned from a fancy dinner, dressed in one of my best pantsuits. I'd let four excited, slobbering dogs out in the backyard to take care of business, and then called them in for the night.

CJ, the group's senior citizen, was totally deaf and nearly blind, but still able to function by following his pack pals. On this chilly winter evening, as the dogs headed for the warmth of the kitchen, CJ danced an arthritic jig in anticipation of the yummy bedtime Milk-Bone he knew was coming and, in his exultation, somehow forgot about the backyard pool.

"Look out, CJ!" I yelled from the back door.

But he couldn't hear my warning or see the watery expanse yawning before him. Down into the deep blue he plunged.

No doubt in his younger days, CJ could have easily followed my voice and doggie-paddled to the steps to climb out, but in his aged, distressed state, all he

could do was flounder stiff-legged and sink like a boulder. My heart sank right along with him.

What should I do? Ideas flashed through my mind: call 911 (about a dog?), fish him out with the pole skimmer (no way), toss him a life preserver (well, duh—he has no hands!). As CJ's black nose went under for the last time, I glanced woefully down at my dry-clean-only suit. It was a Kasper. A *Kasper*! What would pool chlorine do to it? Probably either bleach it out or shrink it to schnauzer size by morning. Sigh.

As CJ's air bubbles thinned out on the surface of the water, I knew there was no more time. Moaning aloud, I flipped off my heels, chucked my watch into a nearby potted plant, and jumped feet first into the gasping-cold water.

I hoisted the mass of sodden mutt onto the pool deck, relieved that canine CPR wasn't necessary as CJ coughed, shook himself, and trotted away. Just as I was dragging myself up the steps with poor drowned Kasper clinging like a second skin to my goose-bumped flesh, the house burglar alarm suddenly shrieked its ear-piercing augury.

The horrible racket made me cringe. What could have tripped the alarm? Hmm. Now where did I put that remote control? Oh no, no, no. I shook my head in disbelief as my shivering fingers retrieved from my pocket not only the drenched house alarm remote, but also my car key clicker. Neither was dunk proof.

Then the phone began to ring. And ring. And ring.

Scanning the pool deck in vain for a towel, I knew I'd better hurry to answer what was surely the alarm company's warning call before the police showed up at the door. Sloshing into the house, I lunged for the phone and skidded on the tile floor, landing on my bum in a growing puddle from my dripping Kasper. So while the alarm screeched and the dogs howled, I sat there on the wet floor, trying to explain the absurd situation to the extremely skeptical alarm company lady.

I felt my blood pressure rise to panic level. Come on, Debbie, *think*! For the life of me, I couldn't remember the code to deactivate the stupid thing, nor could I recall my sister's secret password. Wasn't it a name? One of their kids? Pets? The fifteenth US president?

After futilely trying all of the above, I started reciting the names of every dead goldfish, parakeet, and president I could remember. I had to practically scream to be heard above that confounded alarm. I finally hit pay dirt with the name of my nephew's long-deceased dog. The horrible noise ceased with the abruptness of a guillotine.

Ah, sweet peace. Silence. Thank You, Lord. Oh. Had I even remembered to pray? No matter, I'd solved the problem all by myself. Self-satisfied smile. Smug nod.

But as soon as I hung up, the alarm went off again. What a nightmare; it wouldn't stay off and nothing within my power could stop it. The shorted-out remote from my dip in the pool must've kept triggering the system.

Or more likely, Papa God was making a very loud statement.

So what's a girl to do when emergencies arise and split-second decisions are required? It happens to all of us, sooner or later. And we don't always think clearly.

We sometimes make disastrous choices. We forget to depend on the Creator of all things for guidance, and *trust* that He will indeed guide us. Our lifestyle of trust hasn't kicked in. Instead, we foolishly depend on ourselves—with our limited scope of knowledge—to figure out a solution.

Trust in our heavenly Father is meant to literally become part of us. A lifestyle. An underlying belief system that is woven into the fabric of our being as much as the color of our eyes. Not something we have to remember to apply in order for it to be effective, like sunscreen or lipstick. . .or a remote control alarm.

A good example is Peter in the Garden of Gethsemane, who panicked when Judas brought soldiers to arrest Jesus. Peter hadn't yet learned to trust in the Lord with all his heart and *not* lean on his own understanding (see Proverbs 3:5), so he reacted in his typical, impulsive Deb Coty-esque manner. He whipped out his ear-slicing sword, told three bold-faced lies, and skittered away from danger like a scared rabbit (see Luke 22:47–62). Peter was a person wanting desperately to trust his Jesus but besieged by weakness and doubt. I *so* identify with his impetuous, leap-before-you-look, walk-on-water-until you-realize-what-you're-doing personality (see Matthew 14:28–31).

But sometimes—thankfully—trust triumphs and we make good decisions. Like this very same Peter who later matured in his faith to the point where trust was second nature. Wherever God led, he followed. While imprisoned, he awoke from a dead sleep and, without waffling a single second, followed an angel (*not* your normal jail visitor!) past armed guards and right out through locked gates (see Acts 12:6–10).

I take great comfort that the "before" Peter could victoriously morph into the "after" Peter. If Peter could learn trust, so can I. Just because I sank in one trust plunge doesn't mean I can't bob to the surface on the next. Or the third. Or the eighty-fifth.

Trust: such an intimate form of faith. In its purest form, we shouldn't have to remember to apply it in a crisis situation—it should kick in automatically if we truly trust the Lord with all our heart and live what we believe. Trust should cling to us like a second skin (but not as cold as a wet Kasper). We always have it on and don't have to think about it. It grows with us and we can completely depend on its protection.

Thankfully, Papa God knows that it's a learning process for all of us. He's patiently waiting for our level of reliance to catch up and override our not-so-common sense as we take the plunge into trust.

Even if it means drowning a few electronic gizmos along the way.

> I know God will not give me anything I can't handle.
> I just wish He didn't trust me so much.
>
> MOTHER TERESA

LET'S DECOM-STRESS

1. Can you recall a situation when you took a plunge of trust? Did you sink or float?

2. Do you identify with Peter's panicked response in the Garden of Gethsemane? Or perhaps your trust has ripened to that of Peter's great prison escape?

3. Where do you feel your functional (as opposed to academic) level of trust in God falls on a scale of 1 (low) to 10 (high)? What steps can you take to increase one level by this time next month?

Crossing Home Plate
—LIFE AFTER LIFE—

*Precious in the sight of the
LORD is the death of his saints.*
PSALM 116:15 KJV

It was all my fault.

I had convinced Chuck to come home to celebrate his birthday on Thursday with our family. He'd been at his mother's side for the two weeks since she had been diagnosed with inoperable cancer and placed on hospice at her home three hours away. Chuck just couldn't forgive himself because he hadn't been present when his dad had suddenly passed away several years before, and vowed to be there for his mother.

With nervous reluctance, and only because she appeared stable, he'd agreed to drive home late Wednesday for a pre-birthday dinner that night with our daughter and son-in-law and extended family. Then after I got off work at noon on Thursday, I would return to Mom's house with Chuck, and we would share a candle-decorated cupcake with her in honor of her only son's birth.

But our plans fell apart like shards of shattered glass.

At 10:35 Thursday morning, I received Chuck's fateful call at work. "Mom is gone." I could barely make out the words through his heartbroken sobs. "She died on my birthday. And I wasn't there."

Inconsolable, Chuck endured the most miserable day of his life. My own heart felt shredded. I could only silently plead with God to somehow comfort my husband, while I was racked with guilt that I had caused at least part of his pain.

Later that night, surrounded by a lifetime of memories and his parents' belongings in their too-silent house, we curled up together to watch the fourth game of the American League play-offs between the Boston Red Sox and the Tampa Bay Rays.

You're probably wondering how we could possibly watch a ball game at such a time as this. I must admit, I wondered the same thing. You have to understand that as far back as he could remember, Chuck and his father, a Bostonian, were diehard Red Sox fans (even our dog is named Fenway, after the famed Boston baseball park). I'm not sure how it works, but Chuck's bond with his dad is somehow intertwined with the Sox. Certain elements of the male gender transcend the female capacity to comprehend. We just have to play along.

So on the night Chuck became an orphan, there he sat, staring glumly at the Red Sox game, witnessing the worst-case scenario. The Sox were down 3–1 in the series and had tanked the previous game 9–1. This win by the Rays would seal Boston's doom. So close to victory, yet so far.

The Rays were up 7–0 in the seventh inning when I couldn't bear to witness Chuck's prolonged agony any longer. "I'm going to bed," I announced, "and I really think you should, too. You don't need any more gut-ripping today."

"I know." He shook his head almost imperceptibly, dark circles deepening under his weary eyes. "I just can't leave them yet. I'll just be a few more minutes."

I pulled up the covers and launched a heartfelt prayer—like a high fly ball soaring into the heavens—for my fragmented husband.

And like the pro He is, Papa God caught it. This is Chuck's account:

"People can think anything they want about how all the pieces fell into place, but I truly believe it was divinely orchestrated for God's mercy and grace to touch the depths of my soul when I needed it most. It was a life-breath as I gasped for air from the weight of the sorrow of losing Mom.

"With two outs in the seventh inning, a miraculous comeback began. Batters that had been comatose the entire game sprang to life. Four runs scored, then three more in the eighth, tying the game 7–7. In the bottom of the ninth inning with two outs and runners on first and third base, a screaming line drive flew over the Rays' right fielder's head. Tears streamed down my face when the Red Sox player was mobbed crossing home plate as he scored the winning run.

"I wasn't crying because we won the silly game, but because this was a special message. I knew without a doubt that Mom, too, had crossed home plate safely.

"Just a game? Not for me. It was a touch from heaven. Maybe, just maybe, as Mom entered God's presence with Dad's loving arm around her, God said,

'Welcome home, beloved daughter! If there's anything you need, please let Me know.'

"And Mom immediately replied, 'Lord, I need a miracle down there in Fenway Park tonight. Our son misses us more than should be humanly possible and we want to send him a special message that we're okay.'

"'As you wish,' God said. And it was so."

"Where, O death, is your victory? Where, O death, is your sting?" (1 Corinthians 15:55 NIV). Eternal life is the dessert on the smorgasbord of faith. Walking hand in hand with our heavenly Father during our limited days on earth is marvelous enough, but the promise of being in His presence forever in heaven is almost beyond comprehension.

Pleasure and joy greater than we have ever known. Peace beyond compare. No sorrows, tears, or pain. Who wouldn't want such a glorious beginning to look forward to when our time on earth is at an end?

Dear sister, if you haven't yet taken the step of accepting Jesus Christ as your Lord and Savior, *please* consider doing so now. It's the most important decision you'll ever make. Reserve your spot in heaven and begin your incredible journey of faith right this very minute. It's as simple as ABC.

A: Admitting that we've done wrong things and that our hearts are dirty, smudged, unclean. Many of us can't stand living with unclean houses, but we live with unclean hearts. At first glance, our hearts may look reasonably clean, but God who knows all things sees the grimy corners, beneath the refrigerator, the locked closets where we hide our envy, selfishness, critical spirits.

We all need a spring cleaning of the soul.

> Since we've compiled this long and sorry record as sinners. . .and proved that we are utterly incapable of living the glorious lives God wills for us, God did it for us. Out of sheer generosity he put us in right standing with himself. A pure gift. He got us out of the mess we're in and restored us to where he always wanted us to be. And he did it by means of Jesus Christ. (Romans 3:23–24 MSG)

Yes, we *all* have sinned. You know, in this day and age when anything goes, it's hard to know what sin is. *Sin* is actually an archery term that means "missing the mark." The bull's-eye is the perfect you, the best you can possibly be using everything within you. But everything within you isn't enough. What happens when we miss the mark? Sin. Those sins pile up and dirty our hearts. How do we get rid of them? How do we clean our souls?

B: Believing that Jesus died for our sins and rose from the grave.

> You were dead because of your sins and because your sinful nature was not yet cut away. Then God made you alive with Christ, for he forgave all our sins. He canceled the record of the charges against us and took it away by nailing it to the cross. (Colossians 2:13–14 NLT)

God sent His only Son, the only perfect person who ever lived, to die in our place. Someone had to pay the price for us falling short, for missing the mark. Jesus willingly accepted our payment and then rose again from the dead, victorious over death for all time so that we who believe might share in eternal life.

C: Committing our lives to Him. It's not about religion. It's about relationship. "If you confess with your mouth Jesus as Lord, and believe in your heart that God raised Him from the dead, you will be saved" (Romans 10:9 NASB). When we turn control of our lives over to our Lord, everlasting life is ours. Not just the promise of heaven when we die, but the glorious opportunity to live our lives walking intimately beside our Abba Father, our Papa God, *today.*

God pours life into death and death into life without a drop being spilled.

UNKNOWN

LET'S DECOM-STRESS

1. When did you take the step of accepting Christ as your Lord and Savior? As a child? A teen? An adult? Just now?

2. Isn't the peace we feel amazing when we reflect on the beautiful free gift of eternal life in the presence of the One who loves us more than life itself?

3. Take a moment and lift up your favorite song or poem of gratitude to your Lord for all He has given for you.

Keep the Faith, Baby
—DEPENDENCE ON GOD—

Be anxious for nothing, but in everything by prayer and
supplication with thanksgiving let your requests be made known
to God. And the peace of God, which surpasses all comprehenion,
will guard your hearts and your minds in Christ Jesus.

PHILIPPIANS 4:6–7 NASB

When I was a little girl, my family would pile into our Plymouth station wagon for the long Thanksgiving drive to my grandmother's house in north Georgia. My sister and I sat in the backseat, laughing, singing, and enjoying the journey, with full confidence that Daddy would drive us safely to our destination.

We didn't worry. We didn't fret. We never feared the what-ifs: What if a tire pops? What if somebody broadsides us? What if a cyclone swoops down and turns our car into a gigantic Frisbee?

We had peace because we trusted our father and knew we were safe in his hands.

In the same way, Papa God is our heavenly Father and we can trust that He will get us safely where we need to be. We don't need to worry, fret, or fear the what-ifs.

But as grown women, the what-ifs often steal our peace and add to our emotional turmoil: What if I lose my job? What if someone finds out my secret? What if the group of women I want to be part of doesn't accept me? What if I'm not good enough? What if my children grow up to be serial killers because I was such a horrible mother?

We must remind ourselves that the what-ifs aren't real. That's Satan sticking his dirty, rotten fingers into our hearts and minds to steal the peace Papa God promises

if we depend on Him as our *Abba* (intimate Hebrew form of "father"). Remember, we can't control our circumstances, but we *can* control our responses to those circumstances.

Let's look at some wonderful biblical role models of those who kept their faith despite horrible circumstances that seemed anything but fair.

Job lost his ten children, all his earthly possessions, and was covered with festering, oozing boils from head to toe. All he had left was his bitter wife. Mrs. Job lost sight of all God had done and focused only on what He didn't do. Despite the fact that she urged her husband to "curse God and die" (Job 2:9 NASB), Job didn't.

His response? "I *know* that my Redeemer lives" (Job 19:25 NASB, emphasis mine).

As a child, Joseph was betrayed by his jealous brothers and sold as a slave in a foreign land. He chose to follow God even though everything appeared to be going wrong. He worked for years to earn his master's trust and become head slave in the household. Then Joe's master's lusty wife falsely accused him of attempted rape. Joe ended up in prison for two long years, where he worked his way up to head prisoner, only to be forgotten and left to languish by the palace employee he'd helped get out of prison.

But Joseph clung to his belief that God had a plan for his life. And what a marvelous surprise ending he had in store! (Read Genesis 45.)

Hannah not only had to share her husband with another woman, but she was barren—a public disgrace in her day. For many years, she endured the taunting of "the other woman," which caused her constant tears and, no doubt, depression. But she kept on praying until God mercifully blessed her with her heart's desire, a baby boy. Hannah's child grew up to become the mighty prophet Samuel (see 1 Samuel 1).

And certainly we don't want to forget our most important example, Jesus Christ. Jesus is not just our Messiah, Prince of Peace, and Savior, He's our role model as a human facing real, heart-slamming adversity, our "God in a bod."

Right after Jesus assured His followers that, although His death was imminent, He wouldn't desert them but would always be with them through the comfort and guidance of the Holy Spirit, He gave the best parting gift ever: "I am leaving you with a gift—peace of mind and heart. And the peace I give is a gift the world cannot give. So don't be troubled or afraid" (John 14:27 NLT).

Did you catch that? All peace isn't created equal. The world's peace is based on the absence of conflict; God's peace comes in the midst of conflict. So we *don't* have to be troubled or afraid.

May I share my acronym for PEACE with you? It's easy to remember and oh so helpful when your hands are feverishly gripping those last few hairs on your head and getting ready to yank.

P: Placing
E: Each
A: Aggravation at
C: Christ's feet. . .
E: Expectantly!

If we don't look up for Papa God's help, if we keep our eyes trained downward on our circumstances, we will eventually fall into hopelessness and despair. We'll lose our sense of purpose and no longer see hope on the horizon. "Where there is no vision, the people perish" (Proverbs 29:18 KJV).

And, as every mother knows, depression and discouragement can be contagious. Impressionable young eyes are watching.

Did you know that according to scientific studies, depression affects children as young as three? In fact, 2 percent of US preschoolers—we're talking roughly 160,000 children—experience depression to some degree. I find that statistic shocking.

But I suppose it's no wonder with parents like the woman who was arrested for running a red light with her sixteen-month-old toddler bouncing around unrestrained in the backseat while her twenty-four-pack of beer was strapped securely into a seat belt. Yeesh!

Girlfriend, our Creator is standing by with a life preserver as we tread water in the stress-pool of everyday life. That buoyant ring meant to hold our heads above water is our Father's inexplicable, infilling peace. "My peace I give you. I do not give to you as the world gives. Do not let your hearts be troubled and do not be afraid" (John 14:27 NIV).

Peace is not something we just happen to stumble upon because the sky is blue and the birds are singing. True peace—biblical peace—isn't achieved by being

passive; it's not something we casually pray for and then lie there like a handful of dry linguini waiting for the holiness pot to boil and plump us up.

No, it's an active, dynamic, evolving process! Peace is acquired by intentionally handing our heavenly Father our daily annoyances, dilemmas, and burdens one by one, minute by minute. By giving up the steering wheel. By opening that station wagon door of trust and climbing in. By making the choice to relax in the backseat, enjoy the journey, and let Papa drive.

Faith is taking the first step even
when you don't see the whole staircase.

MARTIN LUTHER KING JR.

LET'S DECOM-STRESS

1. Are you ever besieged by the what-ifs?

2. Is it difficult for you to relinquish the driver's seat of your life and climb into the backseat? Why do you think you feel that way?

3. Do you find God's peace elusive? Review the acronym for PEACE in this chapter. I hope you find it as helpful as I have for decom-stressing frustrating situations as they arise.

....

....

....

Acknowledgments

I am wholeheartedly grateful for the invaluable assistance of the gracious people who helped make this book dream of mine come true:

❧ Kelly McIntosh, my sweet and ever-encouraging editor at Barbour Publishing, who has become a dear friend. Forever thanks for sharing my vision.

❧ WordServe's Greg Johnson, literary agent extraordinaire; my very own Gideon.

❧ Chuck Coty, not only my longsuffering husband but head cheerleader, emotional backbone, source of Bible knowledge, and patient researcher of scripture. You're truly the dough in my doughnut (chocolate frosted with sprinkles)!

❧ Amie Carns, DPT, my lovely and knowledgeable physical therapist friend.

❧ The many friends and family members who opened up their lives in sharing their own stories of how, despite everything, they are simply too blessed to stay stressed (please forgive me if I accidentally omit someone): Marianne and Sam Cali, Debbie and Rich Cali, Tammy and Scott Hutchison, Tina B., Cindy K., Esther H., Jan McRae, Ruth Ellinger, Kim Rate, Mary Aycrigg, Laura Field, Dianne Mullins, Morgynne Northe, Cindy and Jim Hardee, Mama and Daddy (Adele and Frank Mitchell), Cricket and Josh, Matthew Codfish, and my dear late mother-in-law, Jane Ann Coty.

❧ Most of all, I give all credit and praise to Papa God, who is more than able to do "far more abundantly beyond all that we ask or think" (Ephesians 3:20 NASB).

Visit with the Author

Deb would love to chic chat with you and share a few nuggets of her own brand of wit and near-wisdom with your church or women's group. Contact her through her website at www.DeboraCoty.com. Be sure to befriend her on Facebook and Twitter and dialogue through her personal blog at www.DeboraCoty.blogspot.com.

Look for *More Beauty, Less Beast: Transforming Your Inner Ogre* in bookstores March 2012, and check out these faith-inspiring books by Debora M. Coty:

Mom NEEDS Chocolate—"A laugh charge and a life charge that's better than a mocha latte" (Rhonda Rhea, author and radio personality). Grab a cup of hot tea and a triple-chunk brownie and join Deb in uncovering strength for the motherhood journey from God, Godiva, and girlfriends.

Everyday Hope—A lovely, feminine collection of 200 short devotions that replenish and encourage in the soul-lifting hope of the Master Creator. A wonderful gift for friends and family who need a fresh touch of everlasting hope for everyday life!

Prayers for Daughters—Brief but power-packed prayers pertinent to the fears, joys, and hopes of girls aged eight to eighteen. Adorable gift books for those special girls in your life who need a delicious dose of daily spiritual encouragement.

The Distant Shore—True love is never too lost or too late. Inspirational historical fiction based on the true story of a young girl's adventurous and heart-warming journey of faith on Florida's remote, untamed Merritt Island in 1904.

Billowing Sails—Some dreams should never end. In this sequel to *The Distant Shore*, Emma-Lee continues her quest for belonging against a backdrop of romance, rocky family relationships, and pre–World War I espionage.